MW01137286

"I have known both Joh many years and have witnessed the contributions they have made to so many families struggling with addiction. John has been a strong advocate for appropriate treatment for individuals and families at a personal level and as a professional counselor at local, state and federal levels.

"Having the privilege of reading about his journey of survival during World War II and arriving in the United States as an orphan, struggling to become a citizen and then dealing with his struggles with alcoholism, is truly an inspiration to all who read this.

"John's story is such a wonderful example of how sharing one's struggles with addiction and life's challenges can be transformed into the hope of recovery for so many. Thank you—"

Jim Forsting, MS ACATA LISW LADC
Director, Recovery Plus Addiction and Mental Health Services
of St. Cloud Hospital for twenty-nine years.

"This is a book that I'm glad has been written. One of my daughters—Erica—and I sat, amazed, for an evening while John described this incredible journey to us seven years ago. I asked her, then twelve years old, to imagine what it would take at that age to endure and persevere under such a set of circumstances, and it left both of us shaking our heads. From the opening description of John's harrowing cross-country journey eventually ending in the United States to his "Catch 22-like" experience in becoming a permanent resident and finally his battle and ultimate victory over alcoholism, this book is an inspiring story. John's memoir is a story of courage, love, persistence, and faith that should be read by all of us who may take for granted the comfort and freedoms we have in our lives."

David Ewald, President, Ewald Consulting

"Have you ever heard of a ten-year-old orphan boy who in the midst of World War II made his way alone from Poland to Germany and once there became the favorite mascot of the 831st Engineer Battalion in the U.S. Army? Can you imagine this boy as a stowaway on a ship sailing from France to the U.S. in order to follow the American soldier he had come to love and admire? Can you picture the life of this young boy detained for nearly two years on Ellis Island before making his way to rejoin his soldier friend in St. Cloud, Minnesota? This book describes the unbelievable saga of John Meers, a man whose story has captivated my attention. The word that stands out in my mind as I follow his adventures is RESILIENCE. You will also want to follow the adventures of John in the U.S. and the years he spent being hounded by the Immigration Department. You will love learning how Sue became his wife and bore him three daughters and how they all became part of John's chemical dependency and additional life struggles. Here is a book that describes both the capacity for endurance and the innate nobility of the human spirit."

Linda Kulzer, OSB, PhD., co-editor of three books
published by the Liturgical Press

"This book is about survival—physical, mental and spiritual. This survival developed into love as an 'attitude of gratitude' grew in John. It is also about Sue—'the love of his life'—who held the pieces together as they slowly grew together. It is with deep appreciation that I say I have known both of them the last thirty-seven years."

Kay Smidt, Retired R.N.,
has worked in the Field of Addiction Services from 1971 and
continues as a volunteer at St. Cloud Hospital Behavioral
Health Services, Elder Network Program.

By His Own Wits

By His Own Wits

A Polish Orphan Finds a Future in the United States

John Meers

Edited by Janice Wedl, OSB

NORTH STAR PRESS OF ST. CLOUD, INC.
St. Cloud, Minnesota

Cover background: Polish Marble © Wojtek Kryczka
Statue of Liberty photo © Kjell Brynildsen

Copyright © John Meers

ISBN-10: 0-87839-305-6
ISBN-13: 978-0-87839-305-3

First Edition October 2008

Printed in the United States of America

Published by
North Star Press of St. Cloud, Inc.
P.O. Box 451
St. Cloud, Minnesota 56302
northstarpress.com
info@northstarpress.com

DEDICATED TO MY GIRLS:

"THE LOVES OF MY LIFE"

MY WIFE SUE

MY DAUGHTERS SHARON, KAREN AND CINDY

AND

MY GRANDCHILDREN AND GREAT GRANDCHILDREN

MY LEGACY – MY FOLLOWING

FOREWORD

By His Own Wits is the true life story of John Meers, who was born in Poland during the Second World War. When he was a very young child, his parents sent him to a Hitler's Youth Camp in Germany. He tearfully said good-bye to them as he boarded the train and never saw them again. Escaping from the Youth Camp, he made his way back to Lodz, his home town in Poland. He found the family home, but strangers occupied it. Here he was, alone in the world, hungry, frightened and homeless, but not witless. He spent days, weeks, months wandering around Poland, barefooted and hungry. He learned that begging for food from farm families was more likely to be fruitful because these families had more food than those living in a city. He learned to distinguish German troops from Russian troops and tried to stay away from both.

Having heard that American troops were generous, he searched for an American base and found one. One soldier in particular, Willard Van Vickle, took John under his care, had small-size uniforms made for him, pronounced him mascot of the base, took him hunting, taught him to play poker, and treated this orphaned boy as his own son.

The American troops left when the war was over. Van Vickle tried to take John with him but could not. He instructed John in becoming a stowaway. The boy again used his wits and managed to get aboard a ship bound for the United States. The description of how he did so is a story in itself, as are many sections of this book.

The author of the book, John Meers, shares his life story so vividly that the reader cannot but experience a real kinship with him. His desire to become an American citizen led him to a marriage of convenience, to joining the Marine Corps, to requesting being at the front line during the Korean War. When he finally is pronounced a legal United States citizen, the reader breathes a sigh of relief with him.

There are really two parts to this book. Part One describes John's early life in Poland, his friendship with Willard Van Vickle, and his life in the United States Marine Corps. Part Two is a true-life experience of the disease of alcoholism, as it takes place in the life of John and his family. Over and over again John was determined to stop drinking and over and over again he "fell off the wagon." When his wife, Sue, gave him a choice: alcohol or the family, he knew he needed help and got it. Through it all, Sue was there for him. Repeatedly in the book, John says, "I talked it over with Sue." She made many sacrifices for him, always doing what seemed to be best for him.

There is much anguish and heartbreak in this story, but it ends with a marvelous description of the celebration of their Golden Wedding Anniversary.

It has been my privilege to come to know John and Sue and to be the editor of this very fine book, which needed to be written and which hopefully, will be read by many people.

Janice L. Wedl, OSB, Editor

Contents

Part One:
Escape from Europe and Freedom in the United States

Part Two:
Downward Spiral into Alcohol Addiction and Subsequent Recovery

INTRODUCTION

Never before has one man's life touched me more profoundly than my father's. As the author's daughter, I remember countless times I listened to him tell his story to others, and each time, as he recounted the painful journey with tears of gratitude for where it's brought him, others are astounded. With every telling, I am left in awe, as are those who he's also captivated. With each telling, my mom, my sisters, and I, have encouraged him to write his life. Although the motives for us were to have a written account to pass on to our children, what has transpired is much more than any of us had imagined! To see this book come to fruition has been a dream come true for us and gift of love on his part.

I've heard others describe my father as a man of great strength, of true courage, of prophetic wisdom. In my family, we have described him as a cat with nine lives whose survival instinct was stronger than any adversity he faced! For me, words have never adequately expressed the ineffable nature of my dad. I refer to him as a man of undaunted will and determination. A man of fortitude whose persistence and diligence has helped him overcome every obstacle he's had to face with absolute acceptance, and gratitude. My father has been and continues to be a man with honor and integrity whose compassion for others has often seemed limitless. His has been a shining example of unconditional love and acceptance. After reading his life's account, you the reader, will draw your own conclusion.

It is with great pride and privilege that I have been fortunate enough to have this man as my earthly father. To have been loved so unconditionally by him has been one of the greatest gifts of my lifetime. He has left an indelible mark on my life, and I'm certain you'll not soon forget having gotten a glimpse of him through the courageous telling of his life story. His legacy is one I am proud to have inherited.

Thank you, dad . . . for being the teacher, the mentor, the friend you've always been in my life . . .

I love you . . . forever and always!
Cindy

BY HIS OWN WITS

PART ONE

Escape from Europe and Freedom in the United States

The first fourteen chapters make up Part 1 of this book. In these chapters, the reader will come to know the person of John Meers. He is that unusual orphan boy who uses his own wits to stay alive during the Second World War. Although he is lonely and poor, he does not give up and finally finds himself on Ellis Island in New York where he landed after being a stowaway on a ship headed for the United States.

He desperately wants to become a citizen of the United States and goes through anxious measures to become one. John tells his story so well that the reader experiences his raw desire to remain in the United States. A variety of stories are meshed into one as the reader continues to understand how important it is for John to make the United States his home.

Dear reader, read this book reverently, knowing this is the true story of an honest man, who has conquered the disease of alcoholism and has been a mentor to others who are steeped in the disease.

ONE

Early Childhood

I am sitting here in St. Joseph, Minnesota, seventy-four years old, trying to think of where to start replaying the story of my life. How do I know that I'm seventy-four? I don't. It takes me back to when I was a little child in Lodz, Poland. For some reason, the date, December 6, 1932, has always stuck in my mind. Why? As far as the year is concerned, I don't have a good answer, but about the month I'm almost positive, and the day is correct. I know this because, in Poland, we always celebrated St. Nicholas Day on December 6, and my birthday fell on the same day. I also remember St. Nick coming to the window in the evening, knocking on the door, and coming in with a couple of presents. There were some family members present celebrating and laughing with us, but I don't know who they were. Afterward, we would have some cookies, and then it was off to bed. I don't know my age at that time. I must have been around four or five years old, though. I do remember my parents saying my age on my birthday.

Over the years I have been asked if I had any Negro blood in me because of my curly hair and dark complexion. I

3

have also been asked if I was part Jewish or German. My answer has always been the same as far back as I can remember: "No, I'm Polish." Trying to remember those early years is difficult due to the passage of time. I do recall going to church a couple of times. I was able to say the "Our Father" and the "Hail Mary" in Polish. Even today, after all those years of not speaking the Polish language, I can still start saying the "Our Father" in Polish in my mind, but the rest of the words to the prayer now elude me.

It seems as if I didn't have a care in my world in those early years. My friends and I were not worried about socializing with other children; our outlook was very simple—we played with whoever was around. Polish, Jewish, and German children all played with each other, never giving ethnicity the slightest concern. One of our games was propelling an old bicycle rim with a stick. We had a course to follow; the goal was to see who could complete the course without the wheel falling over. We would spend hours playing that game.

The apartment building where we lived was in a complex of probably four or five apartment houses laid out in a square. In the middle was an enclosed courtyard with a gate that faced the street. At night the gate was kept locked. But during the day, that is where we played. However, we were not confined to just our courtyard. We would go to other kids' places to play as well, mostly in about a two-block area.

I remember one night. We were living on the bottom floor of our apartment. It was a warm night. We had one small light bulb in the kitchen. I was putting some potato slices on top of our cast-iron stove to bake. I remember my mother lying on the kitchen table, screaming. Two women were with her, as well as my dad. I was scared to death, for I did not know what was going on except that I knew my mother was in great pain as she continued to scream. Then, all of a sudden, there was silence. As I think about that incident many years later, I believe that she was probably in childbirth. The baby was probably stillborn, as I never did see it, and I seem to remember hearing later about a sister who had died.

The setting described probably sounds primitive—one light bulb? A cast-iron stove? A table on which to deliver a baby? No doctor? No nurse? All those things were considered quite normal in Poland in the late 1930s. Most people living in the rural outskirts of a city would probably consider our accommodations luxurious because they didn't even have electricity or running water, and we did.

I have no recollection at all of my mother or father working at that time. I do know that they would leave during the day, and I imagine they went to work. We were left in the care of a woman who watched us. Later my mother would return home, and she would fetch us something to eat. I don't remember many details of those days in the distant past. After all this time, I'm left with images only, and there's no one who can explain them to me.

One particular instance that sticks in my mind is something that happened about a block away from where we lived. There was a large water reservoir. I think its purpose was as a water source in case of a fire. One winter a bunch of us kids were playing at the edge of the reservoir when I slid into it and out onto the thin ice that rimmed it. I stood up and took a couple of steps. The ice moved, broke loose and moved away from the shore. When I would try to cross back to the safety of the bank, the ice would move in the opposite direction. I couldn't get off the chunk of very thin ice.

The other kids were running up and down the bank, hollering to me. Someone older must have noticed me on the ice and went to get help. Trying to help myself, I started walking slowly back across the ice, but, as I got to the middle, the ice suddenly broke, and I fell into the water. The cold was unbelievable. I was holding onto the edge of the ice with my rapidly numbing little hands, really shivering in the cold. It seemed like a long time but, more than likely, it was not more than two or three minutes when someone threw a rope out to me, and I grabbed it. They were then able to pull me up, across the ice, and out of the reservoir. If a person has nine lives, I guess that incident probably cost me one of mine. Today, I can say that, but for the grace of God, I might not have been here.

I remember running the short distance home, still soaking wet. When I ran into the house, my mom was there. I told her what had happened, and she scolded me, but I also remember her hugging me. I put on some clean, dry clothes and everything was okay.

I ALSO REMEMBER PEOPLE talking about war and that Germany would probably declare war on us. I didn't understand that at all, but all of a sudden one day I heard the screams of airplanes and some bombs dropping, not many but some. Several days later German soldiers were all over the city. As I remember, they didn't disturb the Polish population much, but they surely did harass the Jewish population. They were cruel and downright brutal. I remember once seeing a Jewish woman with a baby confronted by two soldiers. One of the soldiers grabbed the baby from her arms and smashed it against a wall. I couldn't imagine such brutality. It was terrifying. I was deathly afraid at the horrible sight and ran back to my apartment, afraid they would come after me. Many times German soldiers would go to apartments where they suspected Jewish people were living. If there were Jews, they would load them into a truck, allowing only a suitcase or two per family. The soldiers would grab children who were screaming and crying, while their mothers tried to protect them, begging for their safety. The soldiers would then transport all of them to the ghetto.

The Ten Largest Cities in Poland

Warsaw
Krakow
Lodz
Wroclaw
Poznan
Gdansk
Szczecin
Bydgoszcz
Lublin
Katowice

The general Polish population kept to themselves while this was going on and didn't say much. Actually, they couldn't. Not against the force that was Germany then. Most wouldn't take part in trying to protect the Jewish people because they knew if they did it would mean death to them. But a few people did help. Some hid Jewish people and tried to help get them out of the country. Some paid with their lives for their efforts.

A short time after that, in a part of Poland not far from where we lived, the soldiers put up barbed wire fences that circled blocks of houses and apartments. The regular German Army wore brown uniforms with an armband displaying the German swastika. The men guarding the place were called SS men. They were Storm Troops and were distinguished by black uniforms with a double lightning rod symbol. They were Hitler's elite.

At night we would hear people screaming and crying. There would be raids and assaults and shooting as the Jewish population was being rounded up and put into the barbed wire enclosure. I didn't know this at the time, but now I understand that this was a ghetto where they were holding the Jews to be deported to concentration camps. The time frame is hard to remember. It was either late 1939 or 1940. It didn't take long for them to round up all the Jews in Lodz.

History tells us that, during these raids and assaults, the German generals and officers who led the raids confiscated everything the Jews had. All of their possessions—jewels, money, gold, art—ended up in the German soldiers' hands. The Jews lived under terrible conditions inside the camp while they were awaiting deportation to be exterminated. Of course, I don't know this for certain, but they must have been starving while they were in that camp.

I remember one night in particular. It was dark. Over by the sidewalk, I heard and then saw a manhole cover lift up. A little boy crawled out of it. He saw me and put his fingers to his lips, giving me the sign to be quiet. I took him to be Jewish and, out of fear, I turned and ran back to our apartment complex. I was afraid the Germans would see me close to him and think I was helping him in some way. Evidently he was escaping the ghetto. I don't know if he knew someone who would help him or whether he was just trying to find some food to take back. I'll never know. I do know this much—if any of the German SS would have seen him, they would have killed him on the spot.

I also know that there must have been some people helping the Jews in the ghetto. At night we would hear shots being fired, and people would be screaming. Nobody went out to look at what was happening. It was too dangerous. I remember that as a very terrifying time. One of my huge fears was that somebody would break into our place. If the Germans had any suspicion that Jews were being helped by a Polish family, they would kick in the door and shoot everyone in the apartment. Or sometimes they would round them all up and haul them off to the ghetto.

WHAT I TELL YOU NEXT is difficult. This is the first time, in all the years I've been living on this earth, that I am going to share the truth about what happened to me. All these many long years, I've held this within me. I ask that people who read this story remember the times. Poland was a very scary place then. It was a time strictly of survival. The atrocities around us were horrendous—people were being killed indiscriminately, food was scarce, and human life was very cheap.

Why haven't I told this part of my story before now? Why have I kept it a secret for all these years? Simply this: When I was small and had to fend for myself, I had to beg, borrow and steal just to survive. If I had to lie, so be it. To me, it was a matter of survival, getting out of that situation and into a better one was the only goal. That still doesn't make me proud of what I had to do . . . what had to be done. The following is the story of my family and my survival.

One day, my mother sat me down to talk to me. She was very serious, very firm. I don't have a memory of having a brother before this time, but I do remember my older brother being with us then. My mother told me we were going to Germany together. She cautioned me, saying that we would be on a train, and if anyone came around asking any questions, "Just don't respond and don't say anything." I knew that, if we said anything, someone might harm us, separate us. Certainly bad things would happen. I just know that I was really afraid, and I knew that it was important that I not speak. Not long after that, we were on a train: my mom, me, and my brother. I do not know where my father was. We were on our way to Germany, and sure enough, some men came around and asked questions. I don't know where my mother learned German, but she spoke to them fluently. Then they started to talk to me. I didn't say anything. I just hid my head in my mom's shoulder and they left.

I don't know what town we went to, but when we got to Germany, we went to an apartment. It must have been arranged ahead of time because my mother knew about it and where it was. My dad met us there, and things were fine. However, I never saw my dad in Germany again. I know my brother and I went to school. When I had been in school for maybe three to six months, I had learned to speak fluent German.

I became very sick while in Germany. I don't remember going to a doctor, but I must have been taken to one because I believe I had diphtheria. It was like I was burning up. I would perspire a lot and could not get out of bed for days. Eventually I got better and felt like my old self. As I remember, when I was sick, my mother would get into bed with me, hug me and just love me. I don't remember seeing my dad around. I don't know where he was. I do remember that men were few unless they worked for the police, the fire department, or were in the German Army.

One evening in a large gathering place in the city a lot of people were milling around. All of sudden about a ten-automobile convoy came into the square with Nazi flags flying and the SS men in their black uniforms, giving the Heil Hitler salute. Lo and behold, one of the people saluting was Adolf Hitler himself. He talked to the people for quite a while and then drove off.

These are some things I have never figured out. While in Germany, we went by the surname of Schumpich. My father's first name was Leopold. My name was Heinz, my brother was Harry. I don't know what my mother's name was. When in Poland, we went by a different last name.

A FEW MONTHS AFTER having been in the presence of Hitler, we were on a train again, returning to Lodz. On the way back, I wondered why we were moving again, but it was never explained. What had my father been doing while we were in Germany? What was he doing when we moved back to Poland? Why didn't I see him during the time we were in Germany? While in Poland, we all talked in Polish. When in Germany, we all talked in German. Why all the secrecy? Was my family involved in some sort of clandestine service? If so, what side were we on? None of it made sense to me as a little boy. If we had German connections, why would we be afraid in Poland? Why were we afraid when we went to Germany?

We moved into a house outside of town. I call it a house, but by United States standards it was more like a two-room garage with an upstairs. The main living quarters were on the first floor with one entrance into the kitchen and another into the front of the house that was seldom used. We used the kitchen entrance when coming in from the yard most of the time. The kitchen had a cast-iron cook stove that sat next to a doorway which led to a room with only one table. From the main floor, there was a closed-in stairway leading upstairs where there were two bedrooms.

I know we had plenty of food and never went hungry. The backyard was fenced in, and we had a large garden, though I'm not sure of the size. Such things can look bigger to a boy. There were vegetables and fruit, but I no longer remember what kinds. There was a small gazebo in the garden. One of the things I won't forget is that we had a well just outside our kitchen entrance. All the water had to be lifted out by a hand crank and a bucket tied to a rope, which we then carried into the house. The water for bathing had to be heated on the cookstove, and my mother bathed me while I stood in the wash tub. The bathroom was an outhouse off to the side in the backyard.

One day while I was playing and trying to crank up a pail of water, the handle slipped out of my hand and hit me in the head above my eye. There was some bleeding and some scolding for playing with the well. The cut on my head wasn't deep and most of the damage was to my ego. I wasn't as big as I thought.

There was a fence in the garden that was probably about five feet tall. When standing on the top, I thought it would be neat to jump off and do a flip in the air and land on my feet. The longer I thought about it, the more plausible this idea became. So, I decided, why not, and jumped. I did an elaborate maneuver in the air. The problem was that I landed on my behind and back instead of my feet. It knocked the air out of me for a bit. I became aware that I just pulled a stupid stunt and could have broken my neck had I landed on my head. That was the last of that kind of gymnastics. No one ever did find out about that stunt until now.

The hygiene we could maintain in that place was never all that great. I know we were kept quite clean, but I don't know about the kids with whom I played. One day I was scratching my head quite a bit. My mother took a really fine comb, placed some paper on a round table and started combing my hair. I had really curly hair, and she had to comb the knots out. It hurt a great deal, and I remember I cried. As she worked through knots and kept combing my hair, lice would drop out onto the piece of paper. I know she washed my head but I don't know if she used anything else besides soap. I think the soap we had was made mostly out of lye. It probably killed anything left on my head. I must have been about nine years old at the time.

What my mother did for income at this time, I have no idea, but I do know she worked away from home. I don't know what my father did for a living either. I do know he would get on a bicycle, ride off in the morning and be back in the evening. On a few occasions he put me on my bicycle, and I would go with him. He would stop to talk to people along the way, but I still didn't know what he was doing. At that time, it seemed to be a happy life because we were out of the city, and I didn't see what was going on there anymore. All I know is that the ghetto had been emptied out, and no one was there. Looking back today, I assume those people had been taken to a concentration camp.

I remember my brother going back and forth to school. He was quite a bit older and bigger than I. While I don't have many memories of him, I do recall the day the two of us, with four or five other kids, were out by a pond close to our house. It was in a field, and we would go there to swim, only I really couldn't swim. So on this occasion I found myself in water over my head. I don't know if I got a cramp or what, but I was screaming, and my brother came out, grabbed me and brought me back onto shore. I don't remember ever going back into that swimming hole after that.

One day I heard my mother in a heated argument with my brother. She was screaming at him and finally slapped him. Within a couple of days he was gone. I never saw him again. I don't really know what happened. I think he went to fight in the war, but I don't know what side he joined.

During the day when my mother was working, she had a Polish girl come and watch over me. The girl would have a meal ready when my mother arrived home. We always were careful to speak Polish when she was around. My playmates during this time were all Polish, and there were no German children around, as I recall. I had to speak only Polish.

It must have been 1942 or 1943 and, in the world of a little boy, life seemed great. My mom was home every night, and my dad was home most nights. My dad would let me get into bed with him in the morning, and we would lie there together. He would play multiplication games with me. We did that a lot, and it led me to become really good at math. I could add numbers in my head about as fast as someone could give them to me. That skill was very useful in later years when I was in high school in the United States where I was a straight A student in mathematics. But that was later, much later. Still, those were the wonderful years of my early childhood. Little did I know that they were about to end.

My parents somehow or other must have been working for the Germans because occasionally a German officer, who seemed to be friendly with them, would stop by the house. I know that whenever the officer would come by, they would talk, and it seemed that they were getting really concerned and worried. I never knew what they talked about, but I think they were discussing the war, how it was not going well, how the Russian front was collapsing. My dad may have been working for the Poles in a clandestine position as well. I just don't know. I must have been about ten years old by this time, and my parents then just didn't spend a lot of time explaining things to me because I was a boy, certainly not matters so serious as this.

TWO

German Youth Camp

It was about that time my parents told me I was going to leave for camp. I didn't know what they were talking about or to what kind of a camp I was going. I remember my mother saying it was a German Youth Camp, something about Hitler's youth. I remember crying a lot and saying I didn't want to go. Finally, they insisted I had to go, and, on the appointed day, I was summarily put on a train and sent to this camp. I can't remember where it was other than it was out in the country somewhere and a long way from where we lived. When I got off the train, somebody met me to take me the rest of the way.

At camp, I found myself with many little boys about my age. Two women ran the camp. They were quite rigid. They also didn't seem to like us very much. They were always yelling and screaming at us. We learned things about Hitler, about how great a man he was. I guess they were trying to indoctrinate us into believing that the Germans were the superior race, I don't know. Whatever they were trying to teach us, it didn't seem to go over very well with most of the kids there. I know it didn't with me, and camp was more like a prison than anything else.

After being at the camp for a while, we were made to go out to the railroad tracks to work, shoveling rocks onto the tracks and other sorts of physical labor. Every day they would take some time out to teach us the alphabet. We also had a play time as well where we could run around and do just about anything we wanted to. I know bedtime was set to be when it got dark. I recall saying quite a few prayers before going to bed. All the prayers I said during those needy times were a plea for help. It never crossed my mind to offer a prayer of thanksgiving or praise.

Looking back on that camp experience, I believe the reason there were no men present in the camp is that they were all called up to fight the war, and the program for the camp was put on hold. I believe the two women were there to see that we got fed and to help make us available for work when needed. The food we got was a lot of potatoes, greens of some sort, soup, and very little meat. We also got bread that was dark brown and was really heavy. As I recall, I think we got two slices a day.

I remember clearly being homesick. I wanted to see my mom, and I just didn't understand why she would send me away from her. I felt as if I had been deserted. I felt as if I was in this world pretty much on my own. I was a very sad boy. All the time I was there, I don't remember ever receiving a letter or a note or any kind of a message from my mother or my father, and I never saw them again.

Years later I have come to understand that my parents thought they were sending me to a safe place. Today I understand that many parents sent their children to live with people out in the country and paid them their life savings so their children would be safe and cared for until after the war. Even though it was a well-intended method utilized by parents, many of those children were used as slaves and unspeakable atrocities were committed on many of them. Some of these children vanished and were never seen again.

With the Germans being defeated in Russia and driven back into Germany by the Russians, the Polish people were facing atrocities perpetrated by the Russians about as bad as those committed by the Germans. The well-documented and televised atrocities during those years are indisputable.

THREE

Escape from Youth Camp

After being at the camp for about nine months, I saw many planes far up in the sky, it seemed there was no end to them. I later learned they were the Americans. Evidently we were not too far away from a city because we could hear some of the bombs being dropped. It was a terrifying time. One day close to evening, but before dark, the planes returned and dropped bombs near the camp. One happened to hit the fence encircling our camp, and some of us took off and ran out of there. I didn't know where I was going, but I know I just wanted to get away from there, away from the cruel women, the work and the forced lessons of Hitler.

I made my way out to the road and started walking. Very quickly I realized that being away from the youth camp, though very desirable, left me at a huge disadvantage. I had no food, no shelter, no one to care for me. I was alone and scared, and very soon, I was hungry. There was no food. All I could do was keep walking. I finally reached a city I think it was Dresden, Germany. The city was pretty much obliterated, obviously the target of some of the bombers. Some houses still stood, but, as far as any factories or those kinds of buildings, there was nothing but rubble.

Hungrier than I could ever have imagined I would ever be, I begged for food. Finally, one woman took pity on me and took me in. She gave me some bread and some thin soup, though she had little for herself. I stayed there a few days until this kindly woman just didn't have anything left to eat. She told me to go out and see if I could find a loaf of bread or something. So, I left and went looking for food. I went to a bakery, but there just wasn't anything to be had. I stopped people on the street, but no one had anything to spare. I didn't go back to the woman because I knew she didn't have anything to eat and didn't need another mouth to feed. I started walking again. I was trying to get to a place where I might get something to eat, even if I had to steal it. I begged for food along the way, but most of the time the people didn't have anything to offer even if they wanted to help. But then I discovered that, if I went out in the countryside and begged for food from farm folk, I could usually find somebody to give me a little something to eat. As I look back on it today, I think that was because they were farmers and they had gardens and small livestock that sustained them.

I don't know how long I wandered on the roads, but I made my way into another city. I thought that somehow I had to try to get back to Poland. I so wanted to find my mother. I started asking questions such as: "Which direction am I going? How far is it back to Poland? How long will it take me to get there?" During these times, I had to be very careful about how I phrased my questions to people. I didn't want to raise suspicion and have people wonder why I was asking about ways to get to Poland. But with every little hint and vague answer, I pushed on. Slowly, one step at a time, I started heading back home and, I hoped, back to my mother and father.

On the long road back to Poland, I accidentally crossed over the advancing Russians lines. Because I was out in the country, there was hardly any way of knowing when I crossed over. The only way I knew was when I found myself in a city and would see Russian vehicles and soldiers. Then I knew I had to get back out into the country.

It took many days to get back to Poland, days when I was often cold and tired, and always scared and hungry. Trains still ran, and I would slip onto them when I could. For maybe thirty, forty, or sometimes fifty miles, my poor feet got a rest. Then the track would be bombed out, and everyone on board would start walking again. I walked and walked and walked. The soles of my shoes became very thin, then actually just fell off my feet, and I continued barefoot. When somebody spoke to me in German, I would pass myself off as a German. The time spent living in Germany with my family and later in the German youth camp had made me sufficiently fluent in the language to pass myself off as a native.

If I saw somebody heading toward Poland and they saw me, I would tell them I was a Polish kid separated from my mom and dad and I didn't know where they were but I was trying to go back to Lodz. I could speak fluent Polish and I was still just ten years old, so there were never any suspicions why I was there.

I FINALLY MADE MY WAY back to Poland and looked for the house outside Lodz where we had lived. With huge relief, I found that house, but when I rushed in, eager to see my mother, I discovered other people living there. I had no idea who they were, and they had no knowledge of my family. Worse, for some reason, they despised me and threatened to point me out as a traitor. Something wasn't right, and I fled.

I remembered playing with cousins (whose names I cannot recall) in Lodz, so I went back into the city and searched for them. When I found their house, I thought it was abandoned, but

I found my cousins living up in an attic of their home because their parents were also gone, and they were scared. I talked to them, and they said the Russians had taken my mother away to some concentration camp, and they didn't know what had happened to my father. They told me I should get out of there. My being there was as dangerous to them as it was to me. They gave me a little foot-propelled scooter to get out of the city.

I CANNOT DESCRIBE THE PAIN in my heart that came when I realized that I had come such a long way to find my home and my parents and they were not there and no one could tell me where I might find them. I never saw my parents again. I thought my heart would break. I cried and cried to realize I was all alone in the world. It was all I could do not to lie down on the side of the road and give up. It must have been God who gave me the strength to go on.

THIS WAS A VERY FRIGHTENING time for me. Here I was, a ten-year-old orphan, all by myself, dirty and hungry. When I knocked on the door of a house to ask for food, I never knew if I would be treated kindly and given something to eat, or if I would be dragged into the house and made to work like a slave. Sometimes I didn't have anything to eat for several days, and the hunger that took over my belly drove me to overcome my fears and beg for food. I must have been a sight. Dirt and dust from the roads clung to me, and I had very little opportunity to bathe. Much of the time my clothes were dirty. My laundromat was a pool in a woods where I could strip and wash my clothes. I hung them on tree branches to dry, and, while they were drying, I got into the pool and washed the dirt and grime from my body.

Besides being alone and hungry, I feared the gypsies who roamed the area. All my life I had heard how they would steal small children and make slaves of them. I don't know how much of those stories were true, but, whenever I heard a group of gypsies coming along the road, I would run into a wooded area and hide until they passed.

But I survived. I found food where I could, begged for it when I dared or stole it when the opportunity arose. I kept myself hidden much of the time and stayed away from people as much as possible. It was a very difficult kind of existence. As I think over the experiences of those years, I know I must have been a tough little kid, or I would never have survived.

I STARTED MAKING MY WAY back toward Germany because I thought, if I can get there, I might be able to get over on the American side. Everyone had always talked about how good America was and that the streets were lined with gold. It seemed like heaven compared to what I was experiencing and what I saw others experiencing. So, I started making my way out of Poland again, back out onto the road with the little scooter my cousins had given me. I had traveled maybe two or three days when I started to meet people walking toward Poland. They were thin and dirty and looked broken down. These were people from the concentration camps trying to make their way back home. They would ask me where I was going, and I would tell them that I lost my mother and father and I was trying to find them. One man just forcefully took the scooter away from me and started riding it back toward Poland.

DURING THIS TIME, I felt like I was walking on a tight rope. If Poles questioned me, I had to convince them I was Polish and,

when in Germany, begging for food, I had to convince those people I was German. Was I German or Polish? It became a blur in
my mind which I really was. All I was trying to do was stay alive
and not get hurt. As a ten-year-old, I never knew whether I was
on the Russian side, the German side, or the American side until
I got to a city and saw which side was patrolling there, and most
of the time, it was best to avoid cities. I just kept going, using my
wits as I made decisions that, each and every day, could save me
or cost me my life.

I got to a place where a train was running, and I got on. I
boarded it out in the country at the outskirts of some small village. After traveling for about thirty miles, I realized that I was
on a train that wound up in a place controlled by Germans who
had not yet surrendered. There was a forest on one side of the
train and small farm fields on the other. I don't know, but it had
to be close to the German border or behind their lines. The train
had stopped in this rural place with no town near. Everyone
around me seemed to be waiting tensely. Suddenly we heard this
God-awful noise like fire crackers going off, only much louder.
Then I heard machine gun fire and the drone of low-flying
planes. We were being strafed (machine gunned) by American
planes. People were screaming and hollering, and there was
blood and glass all over. It was just mayhem, as panicked people
tried to get off the train and hide out in the fields and woods. I
was trying to get off too, but I kept falling or being knocked
down. People were running over me, and I wound up being one
of the last off the train. I saw a hay stack out in one of the small
fields. I ran towards it along with others. Planes kept strafing us
as we were running. People fell around me, cut down by the
American machine guns.

I was not hit. Maybe being a small boy helped me. I was a
smaller target or didn't look dangerous enough for the gunners
to aim at me. I reached the haystack and jumped into it head

first. I was not the first one there. I landed on top of a man who'd had the same idea I did. And, just as I flopped onto him, I saw his wrist explode. He had been hit by a machine gun round. He started screaming. I was just terrified. I didn't know what to do so I just got up and started running across the field, expecting at any moment to have my wrist, my body explode.

All of a sudden the planes were gone and I lay panting, terrified they would return. After a while, I thought maybe they were really gone, and I made my way back towards the side of the field where it was heavily wooded. I saw a German soldier lying in a ditch by the train tracks. He had blood all over his stomach and trousers—a horrible amount of blood—and he was dying. I crossed the tracks into the woods.

Then, suddenly, the planes were back again. Some people had returned, and the planes began strafing the train once more and firing into the woods. The trees were big enough to hide behind, so that if the planes were coming from one side, I could go around the tree to the other. Wood splinters and leaves fell around me.

The strafing run didn't last very long, only ten or fifteen minutes, and then the American planes were gone. I knew the train wasn't going to go anywhere because, in the last pass, a bomb had been dropped in front by the engine and another dropped on the train tracks. I was back to foot travel. Glad to be away from the train because it was such a large target, I just started walking away, following the railroad track.

I HAD WALKED, BAREFOOT, quite a distance and for a long while, when suddenly I saw a farm house. I stopped there to beg for food, then continued to make my way to where I thought American soldiers were. I must have been walking almost in a daze I was so tired and hungry because I was surprised to find myself in a city. I didn't know the name of it, but I soon saw that it was occupied by German soldiers. Somehow I had wandered back into an area where they hadn't surrendered yet. I didn't know what to do, so I stayed hidden in the city several days trying to figure out where I should go. By listening to the talk on the streets, I discovered that the American lines were actually on the opposite side of the city, and the Germans were facing them. They were both protected and could see each other or at least each other's barricades. Nobody was firing. I knew that the Russians were coming back from the other end. I thought I don't want to be in the middle of that battle and decided, that no matter what I did, I had to get out of there. I knew that, sooner or later, the Germans were going to be crushed. So, I went over to the barrier where the German soldiers were, and I said to one of them: "You know, I haven't had anything to eat in a couple of days, and I'm really hungry. I know I can get something to eat over there." Pointing to the American lines, I said, "What would you do if I started walking that way?"

He said, "We wouldn't shoot, but I don't know what *they* will do to you. They might shoot you."

I said, "Okay, I think I'll take my chances."

I started walking between the barricades of the two bitter enemies. I knew both sides were armed to the teeth. As I walked across that no-man's land, I'm sure I held my breath, expecting at any moment that either or both sides would open fire at me. I took step after step, my knees shaking the whole time, but nobody shot me. I got to the American line, crossed over, and somebody handed me a candy bar. I continued walking, and no one stopped me. They just let me go. I just took off and left the city to its battle.

I don't know how far I traveled or even where I was going, but I know it was quite a ways. I slept on the ground one night and the next day, while I was walking on the road, this American truck stopped and picked me up. Very soon I found myself in an American camp. The soldier fed me and somehow got me some clean clothes, and I stayed there for a while. This guy was really nice and tried to teach me English. I think he was a school teacher. He taught me the English alphabet, and I know he tried to get me to read, but I had a hard time pronouncing the words. I just couldn't understand why one didn't pronounce the "e" on the end of a word or how he got certain sounds out of an "a" and a "u" and an "o" and an "i" and those types of things. The pronunciation was totally different from the Polish or German alphabet.

But, though I was fed in the camp, and the American soldier was very nice to me, I felt as if I didn't belong to anybody; I was still stuck wandering around by myself, with fear and loneliness as my constant companions. Overcome by these feelings, one day I left the camp and started walking again.

FOUR

Befriended by GIs

After leaving the American camp, I walked quite a ways. I might have spent a night sleeping on the ground as well. One day a large truck stopped as I trudged the road. It was another G.I. He asked where I was going and I said, "I just don't know, any place I can get something to eat." I could speak a little broken English by then. There were two guys in the truck. One of them was Willard Van Vickle from St. Cloud, Minnesota. The other was a fellow by the name of Amesworth. That's the only name by which I knew him. He was from somewhere in Missouri. They told me to get in, and they took me to camp with them.

A whole new life started for me when that truck stopped and picked me up. Willard—everyone called him "Van"—got me a uniform made with corporal stripes and said that I would be their mascot, that I was part of their company. I had the run of the camp, and the officers knew that I was there. I went with Van wherever he went. He told me not to worry, that he would take care of me as long as he was there. Little did I know a close bond would form between us and that I would do anything for that man. I loved Van. The times spent with him while he was in

Germany were some of the happiest times of my life, certainly far happier than any moment since I had left the Youth Camp.

One of my first memories at camp with the American soldiers was going to eat with them at the mess hall. There was so much food, and it was so rich that I threw up everything I ate. After being malnourished for so long, my system could not handle either the quantity or the richness of the food. I was introduced to a shower and how to operate the controls. I had never seen a shower before, and I would take a shower a couple of times a day the first couple of weeks, and spend an hour or longer standing under the water.

Van saw to it that I got a ration card which I could take to the PX and buy anything they had. When payday came around, I would go to the end of the line. As the company reached the table to get their pay, there was a box for me there. The soldiers would drop some money into the box and that was my pay. I would go with the soldiers to the PX, and I could get whatever I wanted. I bought mostly candy, comic books, and cigarettes. Yes, that's where I learned to smoke. The ration card I had was the same as the rest of the company; I got a bottle of cognac and two bottles of champagne for the month. I would pick that up, and, of course, Van and the guys would take charge of it, but that doesn't mean I didn't drink any of it. I would go with them when they would go out on a weekend to the recreation hall, which was off base. There a German band played, and a party would take place with a lot of heavy drinking. Of course, with the drinking, fights would break out.

One night a company mascot from another company was there. A couple of soldiers talked the other mascot into coming over to fight me. It didn't last long because I hit him a couple of times, and he ran back to them crying. Another night, Van got in a fight with some guys who ganged up on him and broke his nose. A couple of days later, we went looking for the guy who broke

Van's nose. He took along an army friend of his by the name of B.O. (that's all I ever knew him by). We went to this particular German Beer House, and the other soldier was there with three friends. Van told the guy, "Get up because I'm going to get even with you. Just the two of us will settle things."

Well, the other three guys started to get up, and when they did, B.O. pulled out a chrome-plated pistol. He told the three guys to sit down, that this was "just going to be between the two of them." Van got even and we left.

Another time we went to the club, and I had two drinks of cognac and passed out. Van had to carry me back to camp and put me to bed. As I said, I went wherever Van went. The parties and drinking were all a part of the army life. Another time Van had been drinking quite a bit, and he and I went to a German beer house. That day, we had been rabbit hunting and gave some rabbits to the woman who owned the beer house. While waiting for the rabbits to be cooked, Van got bored and shot about three or four shots into the ceiling. What he didn't know was that the woman was lying down on her bed upstairs, and Van's shots went through the bed and just missed her. We found out later that one of the shots went right between her legs. Van said, "Let's go, Johnny," and, as we got outside, he gave me his .45 pistol, and I shot the big globe outside that advertised the beer house. We went back to camp, and I went to bed.

The following day Van was in quite a bit of trouble. The woman had reported the shooting and damage to the company commander. He told Van to take care of the damage and compensate the woman to make her happy. Van rounded up Amesworth and B.O., and the four of us went to the beer house. Van apologized to the woman and told her that he'd had too much to drink. He then asked her if she would take $500 in script to fix the damage and use the rest for herself. She agreed and that marked the end of the mess he had gotten himself into. I think I gave Van the money because I had won it gambling, and it was for both our use. If I didn't have any money, Van would give me whatever I wanted, if he had it. We just shared everything.

The captain of the company liked me and wanted to take me flying in a Piper Cub one day. I could tell he had been drinking, so I turned him down. He went up by himself and proceeded to buzz the guys playing ball on the field. On his second pass, he was unable to pull the plane up in time and crashed it into the ground. His guardian angel must have been with him, though, because he walked away from the plane with only scratches and bruises, even though the plane was a wreck. I think my guardian angel had been looking out for me as well. I must have been about eleven years old at that time and weighed seventy-six pounds. Chances were good I would have gone through the windshield of the plane and not survived.

Van let me go with him and his crew to their daily work. They would bring German prisoners from the prison to a sand pit. Van drove a six-ton truck and would hook a flatbed trailer to it. There were wooden posts and boards nailed to the sides of the trailer so the prisoners could stand up and have something to hang onto. Two two-and-one-half-ton trucks would follow us. When prisoners fell off, which happened quite frequently, the truck following us would stop, throw them into the back of one of the trucks and take them to the infirmary at the prison. Other trucks were used by the army to haul gravel. The gravel was used in rebuilding the Frankfurt Airport. I believe the engineers used it to make cement.

Van belonged to the 831st Engineer Battalion stationed at Manheim. I believe that's right outside of Frankfurt, Germany, on the Rhine and Main rivers. I had a wonderful time there. The soldiers treated me as one of their own. Whatever they did for their duty assignment, I would do as well. By treating me as one of their own, I began to feel as though I actually belonged to the company. Van gave me a rifle called a carbine. This was no toy, and it was loaded with live ammunition. I used it while helping guard the prisoners. There is no doubt in my mind that I would have used it if one of the prisoners attempted to make a break from captivity. This acceptance and inclusion as one of them gave me a sense of security and importance. I was no longer a lost little boy far from home without his parents. I was not an outsider looking in. I belonged.

At noon one of the trucks would bring food for everyone. We would eat, and the prisoners would be fed and then return to work in the afternoon. Later we would take them back to the prison camp.

I know these days right after the war were not easy ones for the Germans. I know that they went hungry a lot. But the general public had less to eat than the prisoners because the prisoners were fed by the army. The German people in the metropolitan areas had very little food. When the American soldiers would finish eating, the leftovers from their plates were scraped into a garbage can, which also held any leftovers and refuse from the kitchen. Outside camp long lines of German people with bowls formed, and each one would get some of the food that had been mixed together from the garbage can, until it was all gone.

Van loved to hunt. Sometimes we would get about three or four of the guys in our close-knit group and go rabbit hunting out in the fields. The Germans would follow us. When we started shooting rabbits, people would run over and grab them. They would take the rabbits home, clean them and eat them. Rabbits at that time were plentiful in Germany because none of the population had any rifles or means to hunt. With so many rabbits running free, we would go out and shoot twenty or thirty of them in a day. The Germans just loved to see us come because it would mean food for them and we were happy to provide the rabbits for them.

I remember on a few occasions we went deer hunting in the woods. Even though I don't remember us killing even one deer, we sure spent a lot of time walking in the woods. It was a day out, and to me any day out with the guys taking care of me was a good day.

One thing I learned to enjoy while I was over there was comic books. I just loved them and went to the PX often to buy them. I would take them to our barracks and spend hours reading them. I truly believe that I learned the English language from comic books. At first I could read a few words and later began putting sentences together. Of course, talking to the GIs in English helped me to recognize words in the comic books, and reading them was a daily event all the time we were together. I think I was with that camp as a mascot for over a year.

Van wasn't with me all the time because sometimes his group would have to go off without me, or I would go over to another barracks where everybody knew me and accepted me. They would be playing blackjack for money, and I would get into a game with them and play. Sometimes I'd make a little money. I remember one evening I was playing blackjack with six GIs. The game went on for about three or four hours, and I broke every one of them except for one sergeant. I was ecstatic that I was winning, but also fearful—it wasn't our barracks we were in, and I was afraid that someone would beat me up and take the money. Then I saw one of Van's friends sitting there watching the game. I said to him, "Get Van," and he left and told Van that he'd better come because I had won quite a bit of money. Van showed up, and it was only about ten minutes later that the sergeant had lost all of his money. He was not very happy about it either, but what could he do with Van and his buddy right there. That night I won about $800. I gave it all to Van to hold.

Another evening some GIs were shooting dice. I got in the game. It wasn't very long until Van came by, and about an hour later I had made $300 and walked away.

THE MEN HAD BEEN TALKING about being sent back to the United States for discharge. When I heard them, feelings of insecurity and abandonment began to creep back into me. Van knew he couldn't take me with him and soon began to prepare me for the eventuality of his returning to the United States without me. He had saved all the money I had given him to give back to me when that sad day came. He knew I would be left penniless. As he talked about going home, once again I was terrified at the thought of being left alone to fend for myself. All of the old emotions and fears I had experienced losing my parents and home before meeting Van began to take over. I would be abandoned again, walking the streets alone, hungry and lost.

But, even as the talk of leaving left me hollow inside, I still had some fun times with Van. He, B.O., and I got a truck and took off for some town about fifty kilometers away. B.O. had bought a car from someone in that town. I could drive a truck and would sit in Van's lap and shift the gears and steer it. I learned to drive that way. One day Van, B.O. and I went to pick up the car, and B.O. asked if I wanted to drive it back to the barracks. I said sure, so Van and B.O. took a couple of containers of gas off the truck and put it in the car. B.O. told me just to follow the road we were on until I got to the autobahn, then go right and find a place to stop and wait for them if they were not right behind me. I took off, and that was the last they saw of me. When they got to the next town, they stopped and asked a man if he had seen a car with a kid driving it. He told them that he had seen a car going really fast, but there was no one driving it. I was so small I had to look through the inside of the steering wheel in order to reach the pedals and see.

When I got to the autobahn, I got the car up to about seventy kilometers an hour when there was suddenly a loud noise. The engine started knocking real loud, so I pulled over and waited for Van and B.O. About five minutes later they caught up to me and B.O. looked at the oil and metal parts on the road and said a rod had gone through the block. I got in the truck with them, and they said they would come back and haul the car back to camp.

B.O. could speak fluent German, as well as I could. That made it pretty nice whenever we wanted to go somewhere in Germany and no one spoke English. One time while I was with Van, he and B.O. got a week's leave. They decided to go to Switzerland. We took the army truck. They took gas along in army gas containers, and off we went. We rented places to sleep and bought all of our food. We stopped and looked at castles along the way and saw some of the beautiful mountains of Switzerland. It was a great time. I was as happy as could be. Soon we had to turn around and start heading back to Germany and the camp.

We had been back at camp for about a month, when one day Van told me that he would be returning to the States the following week. He told me that he had tried everything he knew to do, and that there was just no way I could go with him. Of course, I cried and didn't quite understand. We kept talking, and he said, "You know, the trains are running between Germany and France. They're going to ship us out of La Havre, France. American troops are being loaded into troop ships there to send us back to the U.S." He said "I'll give you your money, and you hide it. Don't let people see that you've got money. Hide it in your sock or anywhere no one will know that you have it. Buy a ticket to La Havre, France, and when you get there, try to make your way onto a troop ship. Try to come over to the U.S. If you can get there, I'll come and get you. I'll find you." He said "Just write to me," and he gave me his address where to write to him and I told him I would.

FIVE

Becoming a Stowaway

Today, looking back at what transpired that day, I don't think Van had any idea that I would ever show up on the shores of the United States. I believe he said those things to make it easier for me. The odds of a kid sneaking aboard a military ship were not good. All areas around the ships were under constant guard. It would take a small miracle to get on board and hide from everyone. Even for a small boy. Also, when we talked about coming over, he said, "Don't start out right away because it's going to take a while for me to get back to the United States and go through the discharge process. It may take a month or two to make my way back home and get settled, so don't be in too much of a rush to find me over there because I won't be home yet to help you."

When Van left, he put me in touch with a couple of his friends who had agreed to watch over me until I could leave the camp. When the day came for him to go, it just broke my heart. Once again I felt abandoned, alone and scared. What do I do now? Tears were shed that day, and not just by me. I believe that was the only time I saw Van cry.

I still had all the privileges at camp, and the two guys were pretty nice. They took care of me, and after about six weeks I talked them into going down to the train station with me and helping me get a ticket for La Havre, France. I think it was the following day that I said good-bye to them and got on a train. That was 1946, and I was thirteen years old.

Back then the trains weren't very fast. I remember crossing over into France, and when we crossed the border, the train stopped, and different conductors got on. They spoke French and didn't bother me when I showed them my ticket. We kept going, and I'm not sure, but I think it was later on that day, or maybe the next day, when we got to La Havre, France. In those days, I had no schedule to follow, so time was meaningless other than when to eat and go to bed.

After getting to La Havre, I knew I was going to try to get on a ship, and I started asking some American soldiers questions. They told me where the ships were leaving and pointed it out to me. I thought I better make my way over there and, when asked what I was doing by myself, I would tell them that I was an orphan and trying to get to the United States. I don't know if that was the smartest thing to do because I was letting everyone know that I was going to try to sneak aboard a ship. I had no problem with food because I had money, and the money was in American script so that was always desirable by the local population whose money was worthless. American money was where the value was. So, I could buy anything to eat I wanted and had no problem getting it. Anyway, it was about then that I had to come up with a plan to get on a ship. What was I going to tell them if they started questioning me? I figured that they were going to really dig into my background if I got on a ship and made it over to the United States. I would have to make up a story that was believable and true.

I decided to stick with my story of being Polish, born in Poland, which was the same information I was giving everyone when questioned. It was mostly true. I just omitted the part about Germany and living in Germany for a period of time. I didn't say anything about the German names we used either. I lived in fear because I believed if anyone suspected the possibility of a German connection, I would certainly be denied permanent admission to the United States, and eventual citizenship. I never mentioned this to anyone in all these years, believing that due to my citizenship papers being obtained under false pretenses, they would be taken away.

I made my way over to the area where the soldiers said the ships were departing. There was a dock where the ships were anchored. The dock had a ramp like a little bridge that connected it to the mainland. I saw that guards were stationed there and began to try and figure out how I would get aboard one of the ships.

During the war all the gold disappeared. Once the governments collapsed, the German mark and the French frank had absolutely no value. The only acceptable currency of value was the American script that the United States government paid the soldiers. I had script, and everybody wanted it. If someone had script, it made no difference what country one was in—as long as it was occupied by the Americans—one could buy anything one wanted.

I got pretty hungry and went to a little restaurant to get something to eat and rest for a little while. Then I came back and stood by the bridge again, waiting until dark—or earlier if an opportunity arose—to get to the ship. As I waited and watched, occasionally sailors would come off the ship, and the guards would search them to make sure they didn't have cigarettes to sell on the black market. If they had no cigarettes, the guards would pass them through.

After it got dark—it must have been about nine or ten o'clock—a couple of sailors came off the ship to go into La

Havre. They had on flight jackets, the leather bomber jackets with a front zipper, worn by pilots. One of the sailors had cartons of cigarettes lined around his body inside the flight jacket. When the guards discovered the cigarettes, they got all excited and grabbed the sailor. I don't know what they were going to do, but while they were busy with him, I ran across and hid underneath the bridge. I stayed there and waited until the middle of the night. It seemed as if the hours were really dragging by while I was hiding. When I didn't hear anymore activity at the guard house and couldn't hear anybody moving, I came up from under the bridge and walked down the dock where the ship was tied. There was a gangplank about half way down the length of the ship. A guard was stationed there, making sure only authorized persons boarded the ship. I kept on walking toward the guard so as not to arouse suspicion. I didn't want him to think I was trying to sneak aboard the ship.

When I got closer, I discovered that the guard was Polish, and I started talking to him in Polish. I told him I was trying to get to the United States and that I had no mother or father. I told him a guy with the American Army had been taking care of me and was on his way back home after getting discharged. His name was Willard Van Vickle, and Willard had told me, if I could make it to the United States, he would get me and take care of me.

The guard said, "I'll tell you what, I'm going to turn around and walk the other way, and while I'm walking, I won't be able to see what's going on behind me." As he walked the other way, I ran up the gangplank and onto the ship. I was aboard! From there, though, I had no idea what I was going to do.

I had never been on a ship before and didn't know what to expect. I started looking for a place to hide and went through a doorway that led me into some hallways. I had no idea where I was going, but as I went by this one room, I heard people talking and laughing. As I walked by, a sailor spotted me and came to see what I was doing. My heart was racing from fear, fear that something bad would happen to me or that he'd throw me off the ship. As he started to question me, I told him in broken English the same story that I had told the guard at the guard house, that I was trying to get to the United States. I told him I had no parents and that this soldier had promised to come and get me if I made it to the United States. I could tell that the sailor was sympathetic and would help if he could. I became less afraid. The sailor said, "I'll hide you where no one will find you if you promise me that, no matter what, you won't tell anyone I helped you. If you tell anyone, I'll really be in trouble." I promised him I wouldn't tell anyone.

The sailor took me to a room with a pull-down ladder that led up to an unused paint locker. I went up the ladder and through the hatch. From below, the sailor told me to wait there, that he would get some supplies and would be back. It was pitch black, and there were no lights. I tried to stay calm and not panic. It wasn't very long before the sailor came back. He had some crackers, some water, a bucket, a blanket, and a flashlight. He told me that tomorrow morning the ship would be loading with soldiers and leaving. "Don't come out," he warned. I was going to have to stay in the paint locker for at least three days, or the captain would stop the ship in England and put me off. I agreed, and I thanked him. He then closed the hatch, and I lay down on the blanket and went to sleep. When I woke up, I heard a lot of noise and talking going on downstairs. People were being loaded onto the ship. They were getting their room assignments and settling in. I remember there not being many beds in the compartment below me. These were officers' quarters, the better and more private accommodations. I just tried to be real still and stay quiet in the paint locker. I knew I would probably fail in my quest to reach the United States if I were discovered.

When fears would creep into my thoughts from being in the dark, I would try to focus on my reason for being there. I was leaving behind hunger and aloneness. I was leaving behind Germany and war. I was going to a place war had not touched, to a man who loved me and would care for me. These were good things, worth the risk and the fear. But I was also leaving Poland and any hope of finding my parents, and that made me sad.

Sometimes I would turn on the flashlight for just a few seconds to reassure myself that all was okay. It was a little while (three or four hours) when suddenly the ship, which had begun to hum, started to vibrate in earnest. I could tell the propeller had started to turn because of those vibrations in the ship and began to feel the motion of the ship as it got into water with swells. I guess we were on the way. The only way I could tell the time was by the noise downstairs. When it got really quiet for several hours, I surmised it was night time and the men below me were asleep. When there was noise, I figured it was daytime. That was how I counted the days. When I figured about three days had passed and I was out of crackers and water, I took a deep breath and opened the hatch and came down the ladder. When the officers laid eyes on me, there was total silence. They stared at me, looking as if they were seeing a ghost. Then it seemed as if they all were talking at once, asking questions. I don't remember my responses or if they understood what I was trying to tell them in the rapid-fire questioning. I just know I was elated to be out of hiding and out of the blackness of that room. One of the officers got a sailor, and he took me up to the captain.

The captain was very nice and gave me something to eat, some fruit he had in a basket. We talked. When he asked if anyone had helped me hide, I denied having received any help. He also asked other questions, like how I got on board ship when there was a guard at the gangplank up to the ship. Even though

I pleaded ignorance, the captain had known I might be on the ship because one of the guards at the crossing to the dock had seen me hanging around all day, then suddenly disappear. It was then he had cautioned the captain that I might have snuck on board. Apparently, that guard had not seen me run across the gangplank but figured I might have gotten onto the ship anyway. The captain said that he had ordered the ship searched prior to departing but they had been unable to find me. He also let me know that the only way he would put me off the ship was if we should happen to meet another ship going back to Europe, but that was doubtful. He told me he would radio ahead and let the authorities know I was aboard. He said, "Until then, you can have the run of the ship. You can do what you want, and we'll get you a place to sleep. You can eat with the sailors in the mess hall and the rest of the troops on board. Until then, just do what you want."

I thanked him and one officer, along with another sailor, took me over to the sleeping quarters. They brought blankets and showed me where I could go to eat and then basically turned me loose. I didn't lack for company because everyone was interested in how I got there and why I had stowed away. It was about that time that I also found out that there were two more stowaways aboard the ship, and we would probably be going to a place called Ellis Island. I never knew them but their names are found on the ship's manifest.

We must have been at sea about seven days when we arrived in the New York Harbor. For the first time I saw the Statue of Liberty. I didn't know what it was at the time, nor did I know what the statue represented, but I can't begin to describe how great my feelings were. I had made it to the United States. It felt like my heart wanted to beat its way out of my chest. I was overcome with joy. I felt my struggles with loneliness and fear were about to come to an end. Little did I know what was in store for me. Before we went all the way into the harbor, a boat came alongside us, and men from the Immigration Department came on board. I believe they stayed on the ship until we docked, and then they took the other two stowaways and me over to Ellis Island. I began to experience fear and foreboding about being put on an island that served more as a prison than a reception area. There I was processed and put in a large, one-room dormitory. This was not the America I had hoped to find.

The room had a lot of those single metal beds, a bathroom, shower, and sinks. We went through an identification process. I can't quite remember whether they took finger prints or not, but they certainly had an indoctrination kind of interview. They explained what was expected and what was going to happen. Eventually, they told me that they were going to try to find some of my people back in Europe and, if they did, they were going to send me back. So, essentially I was there waiting deportation, and that was not a pleasant prospect.

In my pocket, I had Willard Van Vickle's address in St. Cloud, Minnesota, and I had learned to write a little bit. A couple of kids from Ireland and some other people helped me write a letter to Willard, letting him know where I was. I asked him to try to get me out of this place and not let me get sent back to Europe.

I spent about nine months in that one room and didn't do a whole lot because the room was behind bars. Everyday at meal time they took us out to the mess hall to eat, and then we were escorted right back to the room. Once a week we were allowed out into the yard to play soccer, but that was about it. It was a prison. People came and people went. Most of them were deported back to their home country, though a very few were released to families in the United States. The count of the people living in that room varied. One time I think we had sixteen to twenty kids in the room. Other times there would only be two of us. Then new people would arrive and new kids would come.

But, though our room was a prison, it was not monitored very well. In order to exist, we had to choose sides of whom to hang out with. We had to belong to one of two groups or some pretty bad things could happen to us. I remember one boy was grabbed in the bathroom by four guys from one of the groups and sexually assaulted. They convinced him not to say anything to the guards or they would kill him. The incident was never reported. There were other incidents of this sort, and I had to be very careful. That room on Ellis Island was not a pleasant place to be.

Six

Attempts to Get to Minnesota

After being at Ellis Island for about nine months, someone from the Catholic Committee for Refugees came to see me, and I was released to their care. When I arrived at their offices, we were met by a couple from New York by the name of Mr. and Mrs. Ksieniewicz. This couple had no children and seemed like nice people. I expressed the desire to stay with them. All the time I was only thinking that this would be a way to get off of Ellis Island, and I had it in the back of my mind that, once off, I thought I could maybe find a way to get to Minnesota. Within a matter of days I was released to this kindly couple. I was in New York. The family put me into a Catholic school. I went there for maybe three months. During this time, all I wanted to do was get to Minnesota and Van. Still the people were wonderful. Mr. Ksieniewicz took me to a baseball game. We went on outings and visited their extended family. The Ksieniewiczs tried their best to form a bond between us, but I already had a bond with Van. I felt badly about having to hurt their feelings, but I had other plans. I was formulating a plan to get to Minnesota so I could be with Willard.

One morning, instead of going to school I left home and began by riding streetcars and buses to get out of the city and then started hitchhiking. I made it as far as New Jersey before being picked up by the police. They ran a background check and discovered I lived with a family in New York. When I was returned to the family, I knew I was in big trouble. If I couldn't convince them to take me back, I was facing being returned to Ellis Island. I promised the family, I would not try that stunt again, and I begged them to give me one more chance. They did. They tried their best. I must have broken their hearts. I am forever grateful for their love, care, and concern. However, neither they nor the authorities had any idea of the love and desire in my heart to be with Van.

A little while later, after returning to school, I had a chance to look at some maps and learned how to go about getting out of the city. I found out which direction to head and what highways to take in order to get to Minnesota. Mrs. Ksieniewicz had some sort of coin collection, and I stole about $10.00. I was going to use that money for food and rides out of the city. The family still had no idea that I was again making plans to get to Minnesota. I made every effort not to cause any trouble and did all that was required at school. Once again I would try to get to Van.

This time, my journey began by taking city transportation and hitchhiking. After two or three rides, a policeman in a patrol car stopped and started to question me. I was not familiar with the laws of this country and did not know that the police were interested in helping someone stranded on a road. This policeman was very nice and took me to the police station in Bethlehem, Pennsylvania. For the second time, the Ksieniewicz family had reported me as a runaway. After doing some paperwork, the policeman found out I was an orphan, and an immigrant who had been released from Ellis Island to a family in New

York. The policeman's wife, who apparently was responsible for the inmates, was such a nice lady, friendly and caring. She took care of me while we waited for the authorities to pick me up, which they did in two or three days. It was difficult to tell which department these authorities were from, police or immigration because they were wearing civilian clothes. The policeman's wife took Willard's (Van's) address from me, stating that she would write to him and do whatever she could to help. She cried when I was taken away.

WHEN I GOT BACK TO ELLIS ISLAND, I was miserable. The authorities told me that I was going to be deported. It was the end of my struggle to get off of Ellis Island. I was being sent back to Europe as an orphan. What would I do? I was so disappointed and downhearted. I believed all of my attempts to get to Willard and stay in the United States were futile, as I was not going to be allowed to stay.

SEVEN

A Joyous Reunion

I never knew much about Willard's life in the States, as he was a very private person. He just hadn't talked about that life while he was in the army. Little did I know that, while in the army, he had been corresponding with a girl from White River, South Dakota, a woman by the name of Millie Oyler. Shortly after returning home, Willard bought a truck and took it to South Dakota and hired out hauling grain. He went to White River and met Millie in person. After courting her awhile, they decided to get married and move back to St. Cloud, Minnesota. Willard had not mentioned me to either Millie or his parents, Robert and Sylvia Van Vickle, in St. Cloud. I believe that, once he left Germany, he never thought he would hear from or see me again, let alone receive a letter from me from Ellis Island.

Shortly after being notified by the authorities that I was to be deported back to Poland, I received a letter from Willard. It was the surprise of my life. He explained that I hadn't heard from him because my first letter had gone to his parents' home in St. Cloud while he was in South Dakota. When his mom notified Willard of my letter, Millie, Willard, and Willard's mom began writing letters to the Immigration Department, the Catholic Committee for Refugees, newspapers, total strangers, and Congressman Harold Knutson, attempting to get permission for me to come to Minnesota and live with them. No matter what they tried, it seemed to turn into a dead end. Finally, as a last resort, Millie wrote to President Harry Truman. After writing the letter to President Truman, they saw some results. They received a letter from the Department of Justice, Immigration and Naturalization Service, stating that, if Willard would send the train fare, I would be put on a train and sent to them.

I received another letter from Willard, a wonderful, hopeful letter that said the correspondence with President Truman's office had resulted in making the arrangements for me to come to St. Cloud. They were sending the train fare, and as soon as that arrived, I was going to be sent to them.

Upon receiving the news my immediate reaction was one of elation, my heart was racing. I was jumping up and down, and then I was overwhelmed with disbelief. Was this really true? What about the notification that I was going to be deported? Was that all history, a part of my past that could be discarded?

It wasn't until a few days later when a couple of Immigration agents took me to the train station, gave me the ticket and put me on board the train, that I came to believe this wonderful outcome was real. I can't describe my excitement. Finally I was going to get to see Willard. All the disappointments seemed to disappear. I was overwhelmed with happiness. I went as far as Chicago on the first train and switched to another train for the second leg of my journey to St. Cloud. I had no idea how far Minnesota was from New York, as this was my first exposure to a country of this magnitude and size. I began to see that my attempts to make it to Minnesota on my own had been doomed.

When I got to the United States and was placed on Ellis Island, I was about thirteen and a half years old. At the time of

August
Twenty second
Ninteen
Forty seven

Hon. President Truman
Whitehouse,
Washington, D. C.

Dear Mr. Truman:

We are appealing to you for help in the case of Jurek Mierzowski, a Polish stowaway. When my husband was serving in Germany
he met a Polish lad who had been prisoner by the Germans and es-
caped and got to the American lines and unofficially attached him
self to my husband's outfit. My husband became immediately attached to him and had clothes made for him and saw that he had food.
He was rather fond of my husband, Willard, and began calling himself, Cpl. Johnny Van Vickle, When Willard returned to the U. S.
he was forced to leave the boy but started proceedings for him to
come over.

In April of 1946 we received a letter from this lad, asking
us to send him money or come for him as he had stowed away on a ship
and arrived in America and was being held at Ellis Island for
violating the immigration laws.   We wrote the Immigration Office
but were unable to obtain custody of him as he was to serve 6
months for violation of immigration laws, but after that period they
would not place him in any home until we had been notified first.
Of course, we were never notified and the 6 months had elapsed so
we wrote again and were told that he had been placed in a foster
home and was happy and contented and to abandon our plans for obtain
ing his custody.

Then in August of 1946 he ran away from this home and started
hitch-hiking to our home here in St. Cloud, Minn. But he got as
far as Bethlehem, Penn. and was picked up by police and returned
to New York.   He is now back in Ellis Island but all correspondem e
must be addressed to Hon. Ugo Carusi, Commissaioner of Immigration
and Naturalization, Philadelphia, Pa. This address was given us
by Harold Knutson, Congressman.

It is our every desire to have custody of this boy and give
him a home and love and care a boy of his age craves. We feel that
if he were given a chance he could take his place with the other
fine American lads of America. This lad of 14 hea had such a cruel
existence and why anyone would want to send him back to war torn
Poland where food and clothing is a scarcity, is more then we can
understand.   Perhaps to you we are just a small link in a huge chain
but to this boy we are an important factor. Otherwise, what would
induce him to come to America and hitchhike half way across the U. S.
Surely not just for adventure and notoriety.

Undoubtedly the boy is Catholic and for a time he was in charge
of the Catholic Home Bureau of New York and they refused to let a
Catholic boy go into the home of a Protestant but why should religion
be so important in this case? In a letter from Rev. Komora, of New
York,(he states that it is his decision to have the boy sent back,)
rather then have him in a Protestant home he is willing to send him
back to Poland at least that is our opinion. I talked to the Catholic
Priest here and he said that religion was all that was standing in our
way.

I am enclosing a letter from Miss Doster of Bethlehem, Penn.
which is self-explanatory.

We will appreciate any help you may be abil to give us and I
am sure that if you would take out a few minutes and write to the
Immigration, you would have a lot of influence.

Respectfully,

Mrs. Willard Van Vickle

Millie's letter to President Truman.

49

EIGHTIETH CONGRESS
HAROLD KNUTSON, MINN., CHAIRMAN

DANIEL A. REED, N. Y.
ROY O. WOODRUFF, MICH.
THOMAS A. JENKINS, OHIO
BERTRAND W. GEARHART, CALIF.
RICHARD M. SIMPSON, PA.
ROBERT W. KEAN, N. J.
CHARLES L. GIFFORD, MASS.
CARL T. CURTIS, NEBR.
NOAH M. MASON, ILL.
THOMAS E. MARTIN, IOWA
ROBERT A. GRANT, IND.
HAL HOLMES, WASH.
HUBERT S. ELLIS, W. VA.
JOHN W. BYRNES, WIS.

ROBERT L. DOUGHTON, N. C.
JERE COOPER, TENN.
JOHN D. DINGELL, MICH.
MILTON H. WEST, TEX.
WILBUR D. MILLS, ARK.
NOBLE J. GREGORY, KY.
A. SIDNEY CAMP, GA.
WALTER A. LYNCH, N. Y.
AIME J. FORAND, R. I.
HERMAN P. EBERHARTER, PA.

JAMES A. TAWNEY, CLERK
T. J. POLSKY, ASST. CLERK

COMMITTEE ON WAYS AND MEANS

HOUSE OF REPRESENTATIVES

WASHINGTON, D. C.

August 21, 1947.

Mrs. Robert Van Vickle,   MIERZANOWSKI, JUREL
817 - 10th Avenue S.E.,   A- 6323800
St. Cloud, Minnesota.

Dear Mrs. Van Vickle:

  Your letter of recent date is being acknowledged
in the absence of Congressman Knutson, who is spending
the Congressional recess in Minnesota.

  Immediately upon hearing from you, I wrote Miss
Hurst, with the Catholic Home Bureau for Dependent Children,
as you suggested. Copy of our letter is enclosed. I also
immediately communicated with the Immigration and Naturalization Service in Washington and asked them to secure a
report regarding the case from their Philadelphia headquarters.
It has taken a couple of days to get the report. Philadelphia
advises that nothing will be done at the moment concerning
this matter and that the New York office is now preparing a
complete report. That report will shortly be transmitted
to central office, after which action will be taken.

  It was suggested that we write the Commissioner of
Immigration and Naturalization so that our interest in the
case will be a matter of record, and it was also suggested
that we send the Commissioner a copy of Miss Doster's
letter. This I have done today, as per enclosed copies.
I am going to suggest that immediately upon receipt of this
letter, both you and Willard write the Commissioner stating
that you want the young lad to come to St. Cloud to live
with you. If you wish to adopt him, I suggest that you say
so, and go into some detail as to what you will be able and
are willing to do for him. It might also be helpful to get
others at St. Cloud to write the Commissioner, perhaps
vouching as to your standing in the community and your ability
to take care of the boy. All of these letters should help
in the final decision of the Commissioner. In writing, use
the file number given above, for purposes of identification.

  I surely want to do anything further that I can in
this matter. When we hear from Philadelphia I will advise you.

    With best wishes, I am Yours sincerely, T. J. Polsky

TJP   Secretary.

John Meers has been known as: Heinz Schumpich when his family was in Germany; Henry (John) Mierzanowski in a letter from T.J. Polsky, Committee on Ways and Means, House of Representatives, Washington, D.C.; John Mierzowski, used on an early Social Security card; and, John Meers, an official name change when he was admitted to this country legally, some time before 1962.

my release to Willard's custody, I was almost fifteen and had spent a year and a half on Ellis Island.

I arrived at the train station in St. Cloud on November 19, 1947. It was nine or ten o'clock at night, and Millie and Willard were there to meet me as well as a photographer from the *St. Cloud Times*. I believe the photographer's name was Myron Hall. He was taking pictures as I got off the train. I just ran to Willard and threw myself into his arms. I was reunited with this man who had cared for me at a very important time of my life, a time when I had been in great need. It was one of the happiest moments of my life. I was introduced to Millie, Willard's new wife, and to this day we still laugh that I was her wedding present. The newlyweds were living with Willard's mom and dad because, back then, times were tough, and it was hard for people to make a living. They took me home. I was introduced to Willard's mom and dad and the family I came to love and the place I would call home. The evening was so full of emotion and excitement, I felt as if I were on a roller coaster. I could hardly believe what was happening and hoped I would not wake up only to find I had been dreaming.

We all lived with Willard's parents, whom I called "Grandma" and "Grandpa." They had a two-bedroom house on Tenth Avenue Southeast in St. Cloud. The house didn't have a basement, but it had a root cellar. It had no running water, but there was a well house outside and an outhouse. We were happy. I remember our dinners consisted of a lot of bologna, mashed potatoes and gravy, and bread. That would be dinner, and it was wonderful. To this day, I prefer meat, potatoes, and bread more than vegetables and desserts. Throw in a fruit salad, and I'm happy.

Willard and Millie owned a lot across the alley from Grandma and Grandpa's and were planning to build a house there as soon as they had enough money. It seemed like, in no time at all, Willard was planning the foundation for the new

John is met by Willard at the train station in St. Cloud, Minnesota, November 19, 1947.

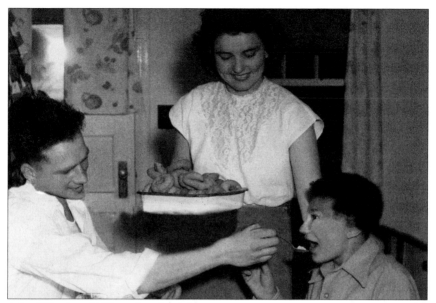

John, Willard, and Millie eating donuts.

house and starting to work on it. In a very short time, the house was completed, and we moved in a home of our own. Grandma and Grandpa were just across the alley. They were the most lovable and kind people I had ever known, and I miss them to this day. They died two days apart in 1964.

Just after getting used to being here, Willard took me hunting and we relived old times. As we talked, I told him the story of everything I had to do to get to him. He told me I was going to have to go to school, and I said I would. He enrolled me at Central Junior High School after the Christmas break.

I started seventh grade in January, and, surprisingly, I adapted very quickly. The math was easy from all the drills I had done with my dad. I had a tough time with English: I just couldn't make sense of the verbs, adverbs, pronouns, nouns, adjectives, and all those things. I just couldn't get them straight in my head. Though I was getting straight A's in math, I was just barely passing in English.

John and Willard in Willard's truck, November 1947.

While I was in school, Willard would drive the truck to go pick up tin at dumping grounds. He would go from town to town and collect any metal or tin he could find in the dump and throw it onto the truck. The following day, when it was full, he would take it to Minneapolis and sell it. That's how he made the money for us to live on. Whenever I got a chance on a weekend, Willard and I would go to dumps, pick tin and load up the truck. On Monday he would take it to Minneapolis, and I would go back to school. Occasionally, Millie would go with us. We just had a great time.

When Christmas came along, Willard and Millie bought me my first bike, and I cried when they gave it to me. I was so happy. As soon as spring came, I got my bicycle out and started riding it. It was one of the greatest gifts I had ever received. Willard had a way of doing unexpected things for me that would help make me feel secure, loved, wanted and appreciated. Willard and Millie also bought me my first car and gave it to me as a surprise gift when I was old enough to get my driver's license.

I finished seventh grade and did well enough for the teachers to decide to let me skip eighth grade and go on to ninth the following year. I finished tenth grade and left high school at the age of seventeen.

When I got to St. Cloud I weighed only eighty-nine pounds, soaking wet. That was after being fed good food by the Americans for over a year before coming to the United States and then being fed well here in St. Cloud. While in school I started boxing lessons. That took up quite a bit of my time. The training for the boxing team must have helped build up some muscle and put on a few more pounds. The boxing team would put on fights at the high school gym. It was an open event, and people could come and buy tickets to watch us compete for the Golden Gloves. Those were fun years. We had to train hard by doing daily road work and come to the gym to train about three times a week. It kept us out of trouble.

EIGHT

Drafted into the Marine Corps

Just before I turned eighteen, I received notification from the Immigration Department that my six-month visa had expired and, because I would soon be eighteen years old, I would be considered an adult. They were not going to renew my visa, and I again faced deportation. Of course, I was terrified and did not want to go back. I was happy here in the United States. The Korean War had been going on for a while at that time, and I thought maybe if I enlisted in the army Immigration might take a different view of my status and allow me to stay. I thought if I enlisted, it would show my desire not only to stay in the country but, if need be, to fight for my adoptive country, and this might prevent my deportation. With that in mind, I decided I'd go to the recruiting office and ask them if I could join the army. When I went to the recruiting office requesting to enlist, the recruiting officer said, "You know we can't take you." When I asked for the reason, he said it was because I wasn't a citizen. They couldn't allow non-citizens to enlist. He said, "However, there is something we can do. We can draft you."

I thought, well, what's the difference? I didn't care how I got in as long as I got in the service, so I told the recruiter to go ahead and draft me. They did! The recruiter filled out the papers, and I was drafted into the Marine Corps.

I was sent to Minneapolis to report for the physical, which I passed. I think they cheated a little on the weight because at that time I weighed 110 pounds when I was drafted, and I think 120 pounds was the requirement. So on paper I became a 120-pound lightweight. Along with new recruits, we were put on a train in a special car for those going to basic training in San Diego, California. Along the way, the train picked up other cars full of guys going to San Diego. By the time we got there, we had six cars loaded with guys going to basic training, and we were pretty much segregated from the general population, with the exception of meal times. At meals we would go to the dining car and be served. Breakfast, lunch, and dinner—we had plenty of food. We also had a little money with us, so we could buy snacks if we wanted. The trip across the country took a while but eventually we arrived in San Diego.

John in Marine Corps uniform, 1952.

At the train station, we were met by a tough bunch of drill instructors. They herded us onto buses and drove us to the base. There we were lined up and taken to the place where we were handed a duffel bag with linens, our shaving equipment and mess gear (eating utensils). Next they took us to the barracks where we were given specific instructions about how to put our gear into lockers and make our beds. Everything was very impersonal, and we were treated as little more than a number. We were lined up again to receive boots, uniforms, and all kinds of clothing which we also took to the barracks. The next stop was the barbershop where we were queued up and given haircuts. It was kind of like sheep being shorn. At each man's turn, we sat down in the barber chair, and the barber had his clippers ready to shave us bald. There was nothing left. We were quite a sorry looking bunch. That was our initial contact with the Marine Corps, and that's how basic training started.

For the next three months we were up every morning early. The drill instructors would take us out for close order drill. This consisted of marching, learning how to handle a rifle while marching, how to carry it, how to place it when at parade rest, what to do with it when called to attention and what the assault position was with a bayonet mounted on a rifle. We also went to classes where we were taught to disassemble a rifle and a .45-caliber pistol. We were drilled until we could take the same rifle and pistol apart and put it back together blindfolded. We would get to the point where we could tell by touch the parts of the rifle and pistol. It was quite rigorous, to say the least.

The basic training unit took kids—we were mostly teens—and attempted to make them into adults, as well as a cohesive fighting unit that would care for one another when it came to combat. We were trained not ever to leave a buddy behind. That was the mentality then and still is. If there was any way possible to pull out a wounded buddy, that individual could rest assured they would be going with us. We would never leave a wounded Marine behind. All the training throughout those three months was to prepare us for combat.

Sometimes we would march up and down the parade grounds until noon, then get some lunch and have a little break. After this brief respite, we went right back out to the parade grounds and marched all afternoon until we became so proficient at marching in unison we moved like one individual, not a whole company. Everyone was doing the same thing, totally synchronized. We came onto the base a ragtag bunch of civilians but had turned into a fighting machine ninety days later. Of course, we were pumped full of propaganda at the same time. We were told we were the meanest, the best of the best, and that we were invincible. I know today that's hogwash, but I guess it was needed at that time.

While we were in boot camp, there was no getting off the base. We were there to learn, and we were there until we finished. It seemed like forever. It felt like a lot longer than it was, but finally the time came when we finished our basic training. We were looking forward to our assignments and wondering what we were going to do and where we were going to go from boot camp. I didn't get to go far. The first thing they gave me was thirty days of mess (kitchen) duty.

After boot camp those who had been assigned to mess duty were taken to a different barracks to live. From there we were taken over to the mess hall (dining room) where we were met by the cooks and given a rundown on our duties. My assignment was to wash the pots and pans and assist the cooks. That's what I was going to be doing for the next thirty days. It meant getting up at about three in the morning to start cooking breakfast. We had to have breakfast ready for the troops by six. After everyone ate, we had to wash all the dishes, the pots and pans, mop the floor, wipe off the tables, and start cooking the meal for lunch. That process would repeat itself as we would prepare food for evening meals. When we were finished with that, we cleaned up again. By that time it was probably ten o'clock at night. We would go straight to our barracks and fall into bed. We had to be back up again at three o'clock the next morning. It was grueling, but we were young and we survived. When the thirty days were over, we got ten days of vacation so everyone could go home.

I got a train ticket and came back to St. Cloud to spend the time with Millie and Willard and Grandma and Grandpa. They told me that the Immigration Department had been there looking for me, and Willard told them I had been drafted. Maybe this had worked. Maybe I wouldn't be deported.

When my leave was up, I went back to California and reported to Camp Pendleton, my next duty assignment. The first chance I got after returning to Camp Pendleton, I went to San Diego to the Immigration Department. I told the officer I understood that they had been looking for me, and the reason I hadn't reported earlier was because I was drafted into the Marine Corps and was doing my mandatory tour in boot camp. I let them know I had not been allowed off base during that time. I explained that I was now stationed at Camp Pendleton, undergoing combat training.

The Immigration officer explained that my being in the Marine Corps made no difference, as the Marine Corps didn't have any claim to me. Only the Immigration Department had authority over me. He said they would check into the matter and then be back in touch with me. He explained that my six-month visa had expired, and they would be starting deportation proceedings.

I was devastated and frightened. All the old insecurities and uncertainties began creeping into my life once again. As I went back to camp, I thought I'd wait to see what was going on and, while waiting, I would continue with my training. What else could I do? For sixty to ninety days, I didn't hear anything, but then I got a letter from the Immigration Department stating that I should report to them. The letter in hand, I went to San Diego and reported to them, as requested. They told me they were going to start deportation proceedings, and, as soon as the paper work was in place, they would come to the base and place me in their custody.

After receiving that information I started exploring various options and schemes as to how I could stay in the United States. I decided I would go to any lengths, no matter what it took, to avoid deportation. After looking at various scenarios, only one seemed to have the guarantee of thwarting the Immigration Department's plan of my deportation.

When I went back to base, I decided to see my commanding officer. I told him what was going on and asked that he transfer me to an outfit going to Korea. My thought was that, maybe, if I went to Korea and into combat, there was a possibility my immigration status might be changed after fighting for this country. My commanding officer said that could be a possibility even though he didn't know the law. At any rate, he told me that while I was over there to get in touch with a legal officer who would be able to tell me what to do. It took no time at all before my commanding officer had arranged for me to be transferred to a company going overseas. I had been trained as a radio operator, so I was assigned as the new company commander's radio operator.

We had three days before we were going to board ship. A couple of the guys suggested that we go party in Los Angeles, keeping in mind that we had to be back in time to make the ship boarding or we'd be in big trouble. This essentially meant going AWOL (absent without leave) if we didn't get back in time.

I said, "Why not?" I thought, "I've lived through an invasion of Poland, a war and bombings in Germany, and now I'm going into combat in Korea. My chances of coming back aren't very good, so I might as well go out and celebrate."

So we went to Los Angeles. One of the guys had quite a bit of money and paid for the hotel room for all of us. We went to the bar where we carried on for two days, carousing, drinking and generally partying. The third day we returned to base and, when we boarded, we were court-marshaled. It seems the Marine Corps takes a dim view of soldiers taking off on their own without permission.

The two guys with me got three days on bread and water in the brig, the ship's prison. After telling the captain my reasoning, that I didn't think my chances of coming back were good, I was given one day on bread and water. That was our punishment for going on leave without permission. We served the time as the ship left port and started across the Pacific. In any case, we were bound for Korea. I had one of two choices—either go to Korea or be deported. Neither of them were to my liking, but I wanted to stay in the United States, so I chose to go to Korea, and I really hoped that taking this incredible risk, one that could easily cost me my life, actually helped. I hoped that, if I survived my stint in Korea, I would be allowed to stay in my adopted country.

The trip over was not much fun. I spent my birthday aboard ship in the worst storm I had ever experienced. For three days the ship was tossed around by the sea. The only food the cooks could serve was sandwiches because the plates wouldn't stay on the tables. That's how bad the ship was rolling. About half the troops were seasick and looked like they wanted to die. The ship was a mess. Finally, after many prayers by many people, the storm subsided. We stopped in Kyoto, Japan, and unloaded soldiers who were going to be stationed there. We also were given a pass to get off ship and wander around town, have a nice meal, a couple of drinks and relax. We had to be back on the ship at midnight. We did make it back to the ship on time and proceeded to Korea.

The next morning we arrived at Inchon, South Korea. When they called my name, I was put on a truck and sent about as far south, away from combat, as I could possibly be. I was sent to Pusan, a little city on the ocean in the far south.

I was there about a week and thought, *Well, this is certainly not going to do anything for my record.* Truthfully, if the Immigration Department was looking for contributions to the country, I wasn't doing anything much more exciting than the mess duty I'd had before.

I decided to go to my commanding officer and volunteer for the front lines. I gave him my reasoning, and he said, "Okay," and wished me luck.

It took a couple of days before I was given orders to report to Graves Registration, which was up at the front lines. I hitch-hiked from one military truck to another until I got there. That was in 1953. Graves Registration received the bodies of the guys killed in combat to be prepared for transport back to the United States. We placed the dead soldiers in body bags, tagged them and got them ready to be put in caskets. It was a frightening experience and helped me realize that, without a minute's notice, I could be dead.

I was angry that I had been sent to this unit because my request had been to go to the front lines. This position, though pretty awful, was still about ten miles behind the combat zone. I still couldn't claim to have been in combat, so once more I made a visit to my commanding officer. This time my request was honored, and I was on my way to the actual fighting area. Both excitement and fear lurked in my heart as I made my way through this country, previously unknown to me.

I went over to Korea in December of 1952, and by early 1953, I finally had made it to the front lines. There was quite a bit of activity going on, a lot of shelling and a lot of North Koreans trying to infiltrate at night. There was hand-to-hand combat, and it was pretty scary.

Our battalion was right on the front lines, in the trenches where mortar rounds and rifle fire were common for much of the night. Sometimes we would hear noise up ahead and call in illumination (artillery fire that lights up the night). The rounds would explode out in front, and the whole area looked like day-time. Sometimes we would see North Koreans retreating as we exchanged rifle and mortar fire with them.

My unit was there about six weeks, and then sent to the rear to rest while another battalion came up to take our place. We were pulled into reserve just to rest up and recharge our batteries. Then we would be sent to the front lines again. I was the captain's radio operator and, when we were being sent up, we had orders for our guys to storm this hill in front of us and take possession of it. The plan was for us to move into position in our trenches. The Air Force would bombard the hill. There would be artillery support as well as napalm (a flammable material) dropped on the hill. We were then to advance and capture the hill. We started to move into the trench lines and, as we were coming up behind the hill, suddenly mortar fire started. Rounds landed all around us. The captain was wounded in that exchange, his spinal cord cut through by a piece of shrapnel. I yelled for the first aid team, called the "corpmen." When they got there, we evacuated the captain. I went back to the emergency hospital tent to pick up the captain's maps and all his information to pass on to the next officer who would be his replacement. I gave the new captain all the papers and became his radio operator.

As we kept moving toward the trenches, the incoming mortar fire continued. Shrapnel flew all over. I got hit by a piece of it in the leg. I was cut, but it wasn't too bad. I hurt my back from carrying the heavy radio, and I received a concussion from an incoming round of shrapnel throwing me to the ground. I was sent to the tent hospital, where they bandaged my leg and told me the back pain was just a sprain and that it would be okay. They sent me back to the front lines. We were there for probably a couple of months in the latter part of 1953. We were due for rest again and our unit was pulled back and put in reserve. Another unit was moved up front. Then we got the news that the truce was going to be signed. Unfortunately for a lot of us, it was not good news. The United States could not bring any more troops over as there was a freeze for six months. Even though we were ecstatic over the cease-fire, we were not happy about not being able to go home during our regular rotation. Unable to

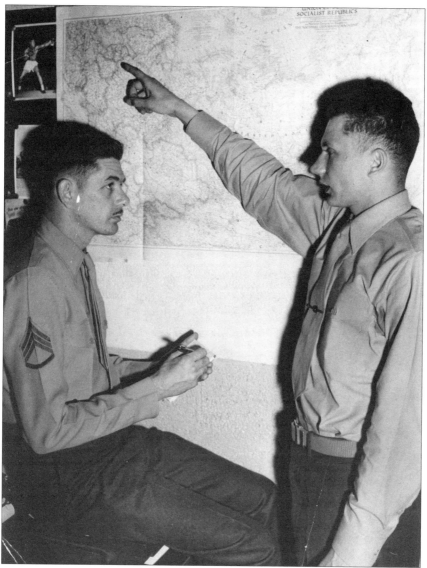

John pointing out a location on a map. (Official Marine Corps photograph)

bring in fresh troops as part of the agreement, the United States decided not to send anyone home for an additional four months.

After we were pulled off the front line, things got pretty quiet. The negotiating teams: North Korea, the United States and South Korea postured a lot, not agreeing on much other than to suspend the fighting for the present. That didn't mean they didn't try to infiltrate and have spies come over and those kinds of things but, for all purposes, the war was over. I was assigned as the general's radio operator. I had the communication jeep, which had all the equipment in it for the general to communicate with any of the company commanders throughout the camp. He would tell me to bring the radio jeep up to his tent whenever he wanted it, which was most of the time during maneuvers. I would bring the jeep to his tent, he would get in. I would hand him the appropriate handset so he could communicate with whomever he chose. He didn't like his regular jeep driver and asked me if I'd be his driver as well as his radio operator. I agreed. So, whenever he had to go to Seoul or to his higher officers meetings, I would drive him there. I felt pretty important, and life was pretty easy. That was essentially my job until we were rotated back to the States.

While I had extra time on my hands, I did arrange to see a legal officer and explained to him what my situation was, the help I needed with the Immigration Department and the status of my citizenship. He was quite positive that I didn't have a big problem. He thought all I needed to do was get back to the United States, find an American girl and marry her and that would make me eligible to file for citizenship papers.

When we got on the ship to come home, it was a joyful time. I was excited about coming back to the United States and doing something about my citizenship. After about six days at sea, we pulled into the harbor under the Golden Gate Bridge. Our stop was Treasure Island, California.

As we were getting off the ship, we were met by a navy band and a lot of people from the base. We were assigned to local barracks while the orders were being drawn up for our next duty. Travel time and leave time was also being calculated as well as expense money for travel to the next duty assignment and money due from our pay.

While awaiting our orders, we were given a few days off. During this time, we had an open pass to get on and off the base. We also were given several hundred dollars to hold us over until all our papers were ready. When we didn't have anything to do, we could go off the base and into the city.

One evening I went to a bar and had a couple drinks. I saw a blonde sitting alone at the end of the bar. I was drinking beer, so I bought her a drink, and she bought me one back. I went over there and asked if I could join her, and she said, "Sure." We started talking, and I asked her if she was married. She said she wasn't and told me she was divorced and had one child, a daughter. I told her that I had a proposition for her. I told her my story, that I needed to be married to a citizen in order to get my citizenship papers and, if she would marry me, I would see to it that she got my allotment check as my spouse. She would get, at that time, about eighty-five dollars a month from the government. Of course it came out of my paycheck, but she would get that while I was in the service. She thought about it and agreed to the arrangement, so we set things up, got a marriage license and were married by a justice of the peace. It was a marriage of convenience.

A few days later I took her with me to the Immigration Office. I walked in full of confidence that my citizenship was just around the corner. I proceeded to report to the Immigration officer, letting him know that I understood the Immigration Department had been looking for me. I told him who I was and gave him my case number. I informed him that I had been in Korea and had just recently returned. I told him that I married a citizen and had been told by a legal officer in the Marine Corps, that in doing so it would fulfill the Immigration Department's requirement for citizenship. The official told me that my service in Korea didn't make any difference, and, as for being married to a citizen, my wife could go back to Europe with me if she wanted. Our marriage had no affect whatsoever on my becoming a citizen. Not only was I not out of trouble, they were still going to deport me, and here I had a wife on top of it. I felt like I had been kicked in the stomach.

I was in a mess and once again had to use my wits to figure out a way to stay in the United States. My new assignment was to Twentynine Palms, California, for additional combat training. I took my leave time and, with my new wife, went to Minnesota to spend time with my family. I found out later that my family in Minnesota didn't think too much of my new wife. After my leave was over, I reported back to Twentynine Palms, California. I left my wife back in San Francisco because where I was stationed is out in the desert. I didn't count the palms, but if there were twenty-nine, there certainly wasn't anything else.

NINE

AWOL to Avoid Deportation

I was being backed into a corner by the Immigration Department and felt the old feelings of fear and the need for survival at all costs creeping back in and taking over. I had decided that no matter what, I was not going to allow myself to be deported without a fight. While at Twentynine Palms, I made friends with one of the marines in the company commander's office. At that time my name was John Mierzowski, and, because no one could pronounce it, everyone called me Ski. I asked the marine if there was ever anyone from the Immigration Department looking for me to please let me know right away because they would be coming to pick me up for deportation. He said he would. I think it must have been about two or three months after arriving at Twentynine Palms when one day the marine came into the barracks all excited and told me that there was someone from the Immigration Department there to pick me up. I said thanks, and quickly threw some stuff in my bag—underwear, socks and some basic clothes and I went out the front gate. I was AWOL.

I didn't have much money or a car, so I started hitchhiking to get as far away as possible. I was not going to let myself be taken into custody without at least some sort of last-ditch effort. Thinking that this a was a big country and finding me would not be easy, I decided to stay away from St. Cloud and make no contact with the family, knowing that would be the first place the authorities would look for me. I had a friend from Korea who had been discharged. He was from Cheboygan, Michigan, so I started heading in that direction.

I was in Illinois, and a guy named Bob picked me up. He had on fatigues and asked where I was going. I told him nowhere in particular, that eventually I would like to go to Cheboygan, Michigan. He suggested that I go with him, and he would show me how to make some pretty good, honest money. When I asked how, he told me that he bought watches and razors and then sold them for a profit. He sold them at construction sites, gas stations, any place where he could find people to talk with. He stopped at a gas station and told the attendant to pump in five gallons of gas. Then he showed him a watch and an electric razor. While the attendant was looking at them, he told him he had won them in a poker game the previous night and was on his way back to base but he was running out of money. He offered them to the attendant for twenty dollars. The attendant paid him the twenty dollars, and we were off. When we saw some guys laying cement blocks, he pulled up, got out of the car, walked over to them. He showed them another watch and razor and told them he was trying to get back on his base, but was short of money. He offered to sell the watch and razor for twenty dollars. He had a price tag on the razor alone for $27.50 and the wrist watch was forty-nine dollars. They gave him twenty dollars. It was easy. We ended up selling wrist watches and razors all the way to Florida. I thought nothing of it then, but today I can admit it was anything but "good, honest money." Today, it definitely would be called a scam.

We spent about a month in Brandenton Beach, Florida. where Bob lived. We relaxed, went swimming and then spent a couple of days wrapping and putting price tags on the items we were selling. Bob said we had to start making another round because he was starting to run short of money as well as razors and watches. As we started driving again, he told me he bought the merchandise in Chicago and got both of them for five dollars. When we got to Chicago, we went directly to the place where he bought his goods. They were unwrapped and in cardboard boxes. From there, we would go to a motel for the evening, wrap the items, tag them and have them ready to go for the next day.

The next morning we loaded the glove box full of watches and put a box with about ten razors on the floor of the car. As we started driving, Bob asked me where I wanted to go. He said it didn't make any difference to him where we sold our merchandise. I told him I had a friend that I'd like to see in Cheboygan, Michigan; I'd been in the service with him. Bob said that we would start heading in that direction. We got to Cheboygan and checked into a motel. I started looking in the phone book for my friend's name. I couldn't remember his first name but his last name was Van Pelt, and he was well known in Cheboygan. I found his home number and called him. After we talked for a while, he said he would come and pick me up and we could go have a couple of beers while we caught up on old times. He invited me to stay at his home that evening, and I accepted. By this time, I was beginning to feel guilty about peddling the watches and razors and decided I didn't want to travel with Bob anymore. I told him I was done and asked him to pay me what he owed me. He wouldn't pay me in cash but gave me some razors. I went into another town and sold them all so I would have some money.

I had a good time in Cheboygan and stayed at Van Pelt's house for a little over a month. I found a job in a music store and also went to work part time for a radio station. This gave me enough money to rent a tiny place to sleep at night. I couldn't call it an apartment as all it had was a bed. There was no stove, so I ended up eating out all the time. At least I didn't feel as if I was imposing on Van Pelt and his family. The jobs didn't pay very well, barely enough to get by. I was continually looking out for something that paid better.

While I had been staying with Van Pelt, he had introduced me to some of his friends, and some evenings we would go out and play baseball. After getting to know them, I let them know I was looking for something that paid better. One evening one of them told me that Chevrolet Motors in Flint, Michigan, was hiring, and the job required no experience. He also said I could stay with him until I got a couple of paychecks and could find a place of my own. I decided to give it a try.

I went to Flint and applied at Chevrolet Motor Company. Due to my past history and knowing the Immigration Department was still looking for me, when filling out the application for work, I made up answers to questions. I knew I had to be careful to disguise my past but still make it look plausible. Van Pelt let me use his address as a permanent residence. It only took about three days before I got a notice to report for work on a Monday morning. We would all go back to Cheboygan every weekend. I thought things were going great. My checks were sent to Van Pelt's home, and I picked them up when I went there on weekends.

TEN

Court Martial Proceedings

During my seventh week at Chevrolet, my life changed again. I believe it was a Monday morning. I was at work on a fender line. The foreman came up to me and asked me to go with him. He escorted me to his office. Upon arrival there, I saw two men in suits. They were with the plant manager and were waiting for us. The two men asked if I was John Mierzowski, ID #1251200 USMC. I said that I was, and they then identified themselves as being with the FBI. I was in my Marine Corps fatigues, which was our working uniform at the plant. It was my understanding that as long as I had my uniform on when apprehended, they could not charge me with desertion. Maybe that was a good break. In any case, they escorted me out to their car in handcuffs. From there they transported me directly to Chicago to the Great Lakes Naval Base where they turned me over to the military police. I was placed in the brig, the naval and marine corps term for jail. I asked them what their plans for me were. They told me that they were waiting for the arrival of two military police escorts who would transport me to Camp Lejeune, North Carolina, another Marine Corps base. I was also

73

informed that I was going to get a general court-martial for being absent without leave for 276 days and, that I might be charged with desertion. They thought it would take about a week for the military police to arrive and transport me to Camp Lejeune.

The charges against me were very serious. I was to face a military court that had the power to imprison me for life. Had this taken place during war times, they could have executed me for desertion.

While waiting for the military police to show up at Great Lakes Naval Base, I asked for paper and pen, and decided to write down a short history of my life to present to the commanding general at Camp Lejeune. He controlled everything at the base. I decided that requesting an audience with him and having the opportunity to explain the reason for my actions might help my case. It certainly couldn't hurt. By the time I finished writing the short history, it wound up to be sixteen pages long. Not so short. I thought it had a decent explanation of the problems I had experienced with the Immigration Department, the bad advice I had been given by legal officers in the Marine Corps, and the harassment I continued to experience with the Immigration Department when they attempted to take me into custody at Twentynine Palms, California. Just as I had been told, it took about a week before the military police came to transport me.

The trip to Camp Lejeune was uneventful. After arriving at the base, I was delivered to the brig again, where everyone incarcerated was either awaiting trial, serving time for a short sentence (usually not over six months) or waiting to be transported to a high-security military prison for longer sentences. Our days were routine. After breakfast we were taken outside where we did close order drill (marching) for about two hours, then we had free time until lunchtime. After lunch the prisoners were put on buses and taken to various areas of the base to work on the grounds. We mowed the grass, worked on flower beds, picked up trash on the roadway coming into camp and did general maintenance jobs. We would work until about 4:00 p.m. or, as we called it, 1600 hours. At about 1700 hours (5:00 p.m.), we were given dinner and then we had free time until 2200 hours (10:00 p.m.). That was repeated daily except Sunday.

We were given access to the rules and regulations of the Marine Corps in *The Marine Corps Manual*. In this book, information was available that could aid in our defense. If we had questions about the legality of anything, we could look it up in the manual. I remembered being told by the recruiter when I tried to enlist that they could not let me enlist because I was not a citizen, but that they could draft me instead. I thought it would be worth double-checking the law. I thought that, if I was in the Marine Corps illegally and might be facing possible years in prison, I would request to be discharged because they actually had no legal jurisdiction over me. After reading everything pertaining to enlistment, particularly eligibility, it clearly stated that a person needed to be a citizen in order to serve in the armed forces of the United States. I was ecstatic. That meant I had a way out of the Marine Corps if they would not hear my appeal and tried to sentence me to prison. I read and re-read that paragraph. I wrote down the page and location of the paragraph and made sure I carried it with me at all times. I told one of the guards that I wanted to see the captain in charge of the prison, and he said he would pass on the request.

In the Marine Corps, everything has to pass through a chain of command. My request went first to the guard, then the sergeant, next the lieutenant, and then to the captain. The next day I was taken to see the captain. I asked to see the commanding general and explained that I thought that my circumstances were unusual. I was told that the general had better things to do than to see every prisoner who tried to desert. I again asked if he would forward the short synopsis I had written. He said I could do all the explaining in the general court-martial. I then said, "Sir, I respectfully request discharge from the Marine Corps based on the rules and regulations on page so and so and gave him the article number. If I can't see the general, you leave me no choice but to take the route of discharge." He then told me he would take the matter under advisement and let me know his decision.

The next day a guard came for me and said to bring the papers I wanted to send to the general and that we were going to see the captain of the brig. The captain was much nicer that day and said he would forward the papers and that it could take a week or longer for the general to read them. He did say that I would be made aware of the general's decision as to my request.

While waiting to hear from the general, I received notice that my court-martial date was set for approximately two weeks away. Then, about two days later, I was summoned to the captain of the brig and told that the general was going to see me the next day. He told me to make sure my uniform was presentable and told me to take the rest of the day off to make sure I was ready. I thanked him and returned to the dormitory to prepare for my appointment the next day at 10:00 a.m.

When I got up in the morning, I was to see the general. I was quite excited, though somewhat apprehensive, not knowing what to expect. I had breakfast and then started to get ready. At 0900 hours (9:00 a.m.), a guard came to get me and transported me to the general's office where I was given a seat and told I would be called when the general was ready. At 1000 hours (10:00 a.m.) sharp the general's secretary came to get me and presented me to the general. He caught me completely off guard as I expected someone who was a real hard-nose, a by-the-book kind of individual. Instead he seemed understanding and questioned me about various aspects of my background. He said that when I had been given erroneous information by several legal officers, they had fallen down on their jobs. He also said that there was nothing he could do about the general court martial. He stated that I would have to go through with the court martial because it was the law. He did say he would forward the information I had given him, along with a letter to the court on my behalf. He also gave me the name of a legal officer to see, telling me he would instruct this officer to work with me until we got my problems with Immigration straightened out. I thanked him for all he had done and was excused.

I returned to the brig waiting for the date of the court martial. A legal officer was assigned to represent me and interviewed me once prior to the trial date. He said not to worry; things would turn out all right. That was easy for him to say as he wasn't the one receiving the court martial.

On the day of the trial, I was taken to an administrative building where the court convened. My defense lawyer took me into the court room where we were seated. I believe the court consisted of five officers, none under the rank of colonel. The prosecutor presented his case and then my attorney presented ours. I was called to the stand, and the court asked questions, which I answered. I was asked if I had anything additional to present to the court besides the paper I had written to the general. I replied in the negative. The prosecution and defense rested, and the court took a recess. In about thirty minutes, the court returned. I was asked to stand, and one of the judges (officers) read the verdict.

I was very nervous. These five men were about to pronounce a decision that could affect the rest of my life. With bated breath, I waited. Then the pronouncement. I was reduced in rank one grade and restricted to the base for thirty days. For a long moment my mind clogged, unable to process what I had heard. Then I realized I had gotten a very light sentence. Very light. I thanked the court and was escorted out of the courtroom. I was granted a reprieve.

As my mind caught up to what had happened, I was ecstatic. I felt as if I were floating when I walked, as if a huge burden had been lifted from my shoulders. I returned to the brig only to pick up my belongings and was told where to report. The captain of the brig wished me luck. I was assigned to do some clerical work, which I had never done before. It seemed that no one was interested in the quality of my work but were more interested that I be able to see the legal officer the general had instructed me to see. I was told to what barracks to take my belongings and that I was to report to the legal officer the next day at 0900.

The legal officer did not want to deal with the Immigration Department directly because it would reveal to them my location. His reasoning was that if the Immigration Department didn't know where I was, they couldn't pick me up. I had to give him credit; he tried his best to help me but ran up against a stone wall no matter what he did. When I saw he wasn't getting anywhere, I suggested that I try to see a congressman from my district. Maybe, if there was anything at all that could be done, it could be done through the intervention of the congressman, if he were willing. The attorney didn't think I stood much of a chance. As we talked more, I asked what action he could suggest for an alternative. He came up with about four things and discarded them about as fast as he named them. I said to him, "Why don't you transfer me to Quantico, Virginia," which was about thirty miles out of Washington, D.C. It might not work and maybe the congressman won't even see me, but at least I'll give it my best shot and know in my heart that I tried everything possible." I thought that if I were thirty miles away from Washington, D.C., rather than 250 miles, it would make it much more accessible to see my congressman.

About a week later, I was transferred to Quantico. I was assigned to communications. Our job was to train officers fresh out of Officers' Training School about communications equipment being used in the field. They needed to be well versed on using the equipment because that's what they would be working with in case they found themselves at war and on the front lines. Quantico was the show place of the Marine Corps. It had a golf course and had quite a few visitors from Washington, D.C., people whose primary objective was a round of golf. For me it was perfect because now I was close to the seat of power. My plan was to try to get an appointment with a congressman elected from central Minnesota, and if that didn't work, I would try to see any congressman from Minnesota willing to talk with me.

I took a trip into Washington, D.C. to look around. I found the House of Representatives and learned that my representative was Congressman John M. Zwach, who was from St. Cloud. After returning to base, I once again went to my commanding officer and asked for a two-day pass to go to Washington. After receiving the pass, I returned to the House of Representatives, and asked where Congressman Zwach's office was. I had no appointment. In fact, I never gave the need for an appointment a thought. I was dressed in my uniform, though, which was probably a good thing. Without it I don't think I would have had a chance to see the congressman.

I found the congressman's office and just walked in. I introduced myself to the secretary, asked her if there was any way I could see the congressman and told her a little bit of my story. She asked me to have a seat and walked into an adjoining office. A little while later she called for me to come in. I was informed the congressman had a very busy schedule and that he traveled a lot. I felt very fortunate to find him in his office, and the fact that he would see me was really surprising. He asked me to have a seat and then asked me how he could help. As I told him my story, he would stop me occasionally and ask me to elaborate. He was very attentive and interested in what I had to say and said he would do what he could to help me. He indicated that he would have to devise a plan and would let me know when he came up with something. A couple of weeks later, the congressman called me back to his office. He told me that he planned to introduce a bill in Congress that would help me to stay in the United States, but it would take a while to get it through.

This was the first time since I made it to Minnesota that I had received some encouragement from someone who had the power to change the course of action the Immigration and Naturalization Service was set on accomplishing.

I had some leave time coming. After returning to base I put in a request for leave. I took a train to St. Cloud and had a wonderful time with the Van Vickle family. I brought them up to date with what had been happening to me, letting them know why I had gone AWOL and had not been in touch with them. I explained that I knew the Immigration Department would be looking for me, as well as the Marine Corps. I let them know that I didn't want to put them in the compromising position of having to lie for me or having to give information which could be used to find me. I was trying to protect the people I loved and didn't want them to get hurt or in trouble because of me. I told them about Congressman Zwach and his working on my behalf. I did let them know that he was introducing a bill in Congress to stop deportation proceedings. I also informed them that he was working on a way for me to obtain my citizenship papers, but I didn't know the details of that as of yet. I assured them that I would let them know any news as it developed. I had no need to remain in hiding at the Van Vickle home or keep them in the dark any longer because the Immigration Department would soon lose its jurisdiction over me. The family was relieved and elated to hear of the new developments.

About two weeks later one morning, I said my goodbyes to everyone, took my bag and walked out to Highway 10, which was just a little over a block away from our house. I started to hitchhike. It took about ten minutes before a car came along and pulled over. The guy asked me where I was going, and I told him Quantico, Virginia. He said, "Relax and get in. That's where I'm going, too." What a surprise. His name was Vern and he was from Virginia, Minnesota. It was surely an act of God for which I am eternally grateful—someone who was going to the same place as I was had stopped and picked me up. I would not have to stand on the highway and continue to hitchhike the rest of the way. We changed off driving, and about twenty-six hours later we were at the Marine Corps base in Quantico.

Vern and I became very good friends. He was assigned to the Air Wing and did sheet metal work on airplanes. The following week, I called a girl I had known from St. Cloud. I had worked with her mother at Quality Dry Cleaners in that city. She was currently working for United Airlines in Washington, D.C., and was surprised to hear from me. She invited me to a gathering she was having that weekend with some of her friends. I accepted the offer and went to the gathering on Saturday afternoon. We had a great time. She introduced me to her friends, who were all women. Little did I know that I would fall in love and marry one of the women I met.

Her name was Sue Antone, and she was from Richmond, Virginia. Sue had a roommate by the name of Jan who was from Pennsylvania. They both worked at the Washington National Airport. Sue worked for Capital Airlines, and Jan worked for American Airlines. I told Jan about Vern and assured her he was a very nice guy and asked her if she wanted me to set her up with him on a blind date. The next weekend, I introduced her to my new-found buddy Vern. We went out to a dance that night, and for Jan and Vern it was truly love at first sight. They became inseparable. From then on, I would see Sue every chance I got, and Vern would see Jan whenever possible.

About three weeks later I received a call from Congressman Zwach asking me to come to his office for a meeting. I met him in his office, and he told me that he had attached the bill on which he was working to stop my deportation to an important piece of legislation and consequently had no trouble getting it passed. He informed me that the Immigration Department would not be bothering me any longer.

ELEVEN

Legally in the United States

Congressman Zwack said I was going to be given step-by-step instructions that I was to follow explicitly. When I returned to base, I was called to the base company headquarters administration building. There I was given a packet with instructions along with orders to report to Langley Air Force Base. Everything was laid out step-by-step in detail, with instructions for every leg of my trip. I was relieved of duty at the base, allowing me to follow through with the orders. I reported to Langley at the designated time and was treated like a high-ranking officer rather than rank-and-file marine. Evidently orders had come down from Washington regarding my trip along with orders to offer me any assistance I requested. I was not to be delayed for any reason.

I was given a ride out to a four-engine aircraft. It was as large as any commercial aircraft I had seen. As I boarded the plane, the crew made sure I was comfortable, and I was treated like a very important person. I must have seemed somewhat nervous and apprehensive when the crew members kept assuring me I could relax, that our next stop would be Guantanamo,

Cuba. That evening we arrived in Guantanomo. I was greeted at the aircraft by a marine and taken to get something to eat. He then took me to a small room in a high-security building and told me to get a good night's sleep. He informed me that, in the morning, I would be given a pass to go to Santiago, Cuba, and there I would meet with a doctor who was going to fill out some papers and draw a vial of blood. Then I was to return to Guantanamo.

After getting cleaned up in the morning, I had some breakfast and went to gather my belongings. I was again taken to the administration building where I was given the pass to get off the base and back on again. I was transported to the front gate and we said our goodbyes. I got a ride into town. There I found a taxi stand where a driver was taking passengers to Santiago. He had four passengers, and I was the last. He charged ten dollars each. The roads were terrible. Because of that, we didn't get to Santiago until late in the afternoon. We stopped a couple of times on the way to go to the bathroom, get a sandwich and a bottle of beer and then continued to bounce along. The driver dropped me off at a hotel that was really quite nice. It was used by a lot of ships' officers who came to Santiago either to pick up or drop off freight. The staff in the bar and behind the desk could speak a little English so I could get help in ordering my meal. After a couple of drinks and dinner, I went up to bed.

The next morning I went downstairs to breakfast. After a couple extra cups of coffee along with my food, I caught a taxi and asked to be taken to the address of a doctor I had been given prior to my departure. The doctor spoke some English and took me into his examining room where he drew some blood. He then took me to the outer office and asked me some questions about where my home was, what my address at home was, how long I had I lived there. He then asked me to come back the next morning. I had his secretary call a taxi and returned to the hotel. The next day, I went back to the doctor's office. He gave me an envelope with some papers. I'm not sure, but I believe they were papers requesting legal entry into the United States and seeking permanent residence.

I again got a taxi going to Guantanamo, Cuba, and arrived back at the base that evening. I reported to the duty officer, who was expecting me. I'm sure they must have had some type of tracers on me to know when I would be returning. It could also be that they had corresponded with the doctor in Santiago. After dinner, I was again escorted to a place to sleep and informed that I should try to get a good night's rest because I was flying out the next day to Langley Air Force Base in the United States.

The next morning I was quite excited and full of anticipation in preparation for the schedule of events about to take place. I was given a ride out to the plane and informed that we would be making a stop in Fort Lauderdale, Florida; I needed to have the papers handy that had been given to me by the doctor in Santiago. I was more than a little apprehensive, particularly when told the Immigration Department was going to meet us when we landed. This was new information, as I had not been informed that the Immigration Department had any involvement in this process.

A short while after takeoff, we arrived in Fort Lauderdale. The plane landed and taxied over to a military hangar. When the doors opened, I disembarked and was met by a person in plain clothes. He asked me for my papers, and I gave them to him. He took the papers over to his car, signed and stamped them and said, "Congratulations, you are now legally in the United States."

I must have stood there with my mouth hanging open. I was shocked. The feeling at that time is hard to describe. Gratitude and elation overwhelmed me as I shed a few tears and thanked the official. But I was stunned, too. Suddenly I didn't have this cloud over me anymore.

I reboarded the plane, and about three or four hours later we landed at Langley AFB. I returned to Quantico and reported for duty. Thank God, the "ordeal" was over. I was a free man not being chased by anyone. For the first time in my life, I was in a safe place with no one trying to kill me, hurt me or get rid of me.

It was only much later that I discovered that I was not as free a man as I thought. No, the marines were fine with me, and Immigration was truly out of the picture. On the outside, I was as free as I felt that day. But the ordeals of my life hadn't gone anywhere, hadn't evaporated just because I finally had achieved the right to stay in the United States. How could they? I would come to learn, several years later, that I was chased by my own demons of lies, alcohol, tobacco, and easy money that I had acquired over the years. At the time of great elation, I had no idea that these demons were haunting me. The groundwork had been laid even in my boyhood for psychological and addiction problems that would bind me for years to come.

I never did let Congressman Zwach know how much I appreciated his intervention, though I realized that without his help I would still be running from the Immigration Department. I know, without a doubt, that, had it not been for that man, I would not be in this country. If any of his remaining family members should read this account, I would like you to know what a caring individual he was, a true representative of his constituents. He cared about their well-being and never forgot about the little guy, even a really little guy like me. God bless his soul and may he rest in peace. For the first time in a long time, I felt exhilarated, free and thanking God for His help and for watching over me.

At the first opportunity we got, Vern and I went to see the girls, Sue and Jan. We celebrated with a little too much to drink. Vern told us he was going to be transferred to Hawaii. It was really hard for Jan, as those two were madly in love. Jan just couldn't imagine living without Vern. Vern and I spent as much time as we could with the girls. Sue worked the night shift and, when she had to work, I would stay at her apartment and sleep. When she came home in the morning after work, I would keep her up all day. We would go running around Washington just having fun. The more we were together, the more we wanted to be together. She was a lovely girl, and we cared a lot for each other.

Sue had lost her father to a heart attack about six weeks before we met. We were two needy, vulnerable people both thinking we were in love. I thought I could fill her void as she grieved the loss of her father, and she, even though she thought I drank too much and had some problems, thought all I needed was someone to love me, that I would change and we would be happy. Little did we know how much heartache we were going to go through in the next years. At the time, we were not thinking in those terms. Our focus was on how wonderful things were as we lived in the moment and how much fun we were having. We were together as much as we could be, with little thought about the future.

I had always prided myself on being able to use my wits when making decisions. Even as a forlorn child, I had used my wits to get me where I needed to go. At that time, I never knew if I would live past the day given to me. I lived day to day using my wits to keep me alive. As an adult, the present moment seemed to be the only important thing, and we got as much as possible out of each day. Sue, however, was aware of my insecurities and saw in me something that others had a hard time seeing. She continued to believe all I needed was someone to really love me and felt she could fill that void.

It came time for Vern to leave, and we decided to have a party for his send-off. That evening we all had too much to drink. Our emotions got the best of us, and Sue and I slept together for the first time. The next day the party continued, and we decided to go to the shores of the Potomac River and spend a day in the sun. Vern and I found a washtub, filled it with ice and beer. I think we had a bottle of bourbon in there as well. We bought some snacks, picked up the girls and set off to the beach. When we got to the river, we spread out the blankets, and Vern was going to open a beer. I asked him to wait a few minutes to open mine because I wanted to go swimming first. I ran toward the water, and when I was about knee-deep I dove in. As I did, I felt my foot hit something. It didn't hurt. As I kept swimming, I felt like something was caught between my toes, so I leaned back in the water and looked at my foot. All I could see was some blood and about a four-inch tear. I wondered what on earth I had done. I swam to shore. As I came out of the water, I asked if anyone had a Band-Aid. Well, the girls were excited and screaming. My foot was bleeding badly. Every time I took a step more blood would spurt out of the wound. After much pleading and prodding by the girls and Vern, I agreed to let them take me to Bethesda Naval Hospital in Bethesda, Maryland. They took me to the emergency room, and the doctor there said that two tendons were severed, and I was going to need surgery.

I told Vern and the girls to go home because we all knew I was going to be kept there for a few days. I kissed Sue and wished Vern the best because he was leaving for Hawaii. I was wheeled out of there to an operating room. I believe I was given a spinal block, which made my body numb from the waist down. A curtain was hung over me that didn't allow me to see what the doctor was doing. He then proceeded to operate on my foot. I felt no pain, and it was not long before the doctor had finished. My foot was then placed in a cast from above the ankle down over the part that had been operated on. I was put on medical leave from the Marine Corps and informed by the doctor that for the next two weeks I would be a patient at Bethesda Naval Hospital.

The following Friday some of the patients, including myself, were told that on Sunday we would be going to the White House. I don't remember the occasion. I think it probably was Veterans Day or some such event. I remember there were about twenty of us in wheel chairs, about forty staff, and a few uniformed service men present. There was a large civilian contingent, probably congressmen, senators, and government people. The Marine Corps Band and Honor Guard, the Army Band and White House staff and security were also present. I felt honored to be in the presence of President Dwight and Mamie Eisenhower as they stood in front of the White House. The president gave a speech. There was a picnic and snacks were served along with drinks. The bands played "Hail to the Chief" and then a line formed and we were wheeled to where President and Mamie

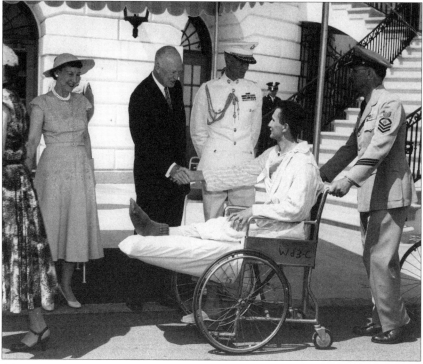

John, in wheelchair, greeting President Eisenhower, 1956.

Eisenhower were shaking hands in a receiving line. As they shook our hand they spoke to us individually. I thanked them and, much to my surprise, the next morning I was on the front page of the *Washington Post* newspaper shaking the president's hand. I would suspect that the picture was picked up by other newspapers as well, even though I have no personal knowledge of that happening. At the end of the ceremony we were loaded into buses and transported back to Bethesda Naval Hospital.

Twelve

Discharge from the Marine Corps

While at Bethesda Naval Hospital, I was seen by a psychiatrist to help me deal with the psychological damage a life like mine was certain to have caused. The length of my hospitalization stretched from two weeks to two months as I was seen on numerous occasions by a psychiatrist during that period of time. The psychiatrist suggested I take an honorable discharge with a pension, which I agreed to do. I felt that to continue in the Marine Corps after being treated for a mental condition would be an exercise in futility. I thought I would continually be evaluated, based on the psychiatrist's mental report and treatment rather than on my ability to serve the country. After about two weeks of waiting, I asked the psychiatrist what was taking so long for my discharge. I was told that it could take up to a couple of months for the pension to be approved. I was extremely impatient and now wanted out of the Marine Corps; I told him to keep the pension and just give me my discharge. This was not a good choice. I was developing a habit of "cutting off my nose to spite my face." The psychiatrist, however, saw to it that I was discharged within a week.

In the meantime, I had called Sue and let her know what was happening. She had missed a monthly menstrual period and was afraid she was pregnant. She came to see me when she could while I was in the hospital but those visits became less frequent, and we were not able to spend as much time together as we did before my admission. After two months and no menstrual period, a trip to the doctor confirmed her suspicion that she was indeed pregnant. We were both terrified and wondered what to do. We knew we loved each other and decided we would make plans to get married.

Sue's relationship with her father had been extremely close, though her relationship with her mother was strained many times. She was afraid to tell her mother that she was pregnant as her mother had not been in favor of our relationship almost from the beginning. Many years later, Sue and I would both come to understand that her mother was concerned for Sue's welfare as she could see that my drinking and background were problematic, and her concern was out of love for her child.

As we contemplated what we should do, Sue and I decided that I would return to St. Cloud, Minnesota, find a job and look for a place for us to live. I would then send for her, and she would come to Minnesota where we would be married. Sue's mother agreed to our plan. In those days, if a young girl became pregnant without being married, it was a disgrace for the family; it was better if the girl went away to have her baby.

On October 19, 1956, after four years and ten months as a marine, I was given an honorable discharge from the Marine Corps. I was given travel pay home and mustering out pay, which is discharge pay. I believe it was prorated and calculated based on how many days of the month were served before discharge, plus an amount for every year of service in the Marine Corps.

I spent a couple of days with Sue and Jan before proceeding on to St. Cloud. We missed Vern, as he was in Okinawa. Jan and Vern were talking about getting married when he returned to the United States.

These are very difficult areas of my life for me to write about. My thoughts and actions for the next few years were certainly not character building. Even though the intent was good, the actions didn't match the intent. Often I would need to use my own wits to get through another day.

When the day came for me to leave for St. Cloud, Sue and I said our goodbyes, shed quite a few tears, and I promised to send for her as soon as possible.

A couple of days later, I arrived in St. Cloud. It was an exciting and happy reunion with Willard, Millie, and Grandma and Grandpa Van Vickle. We spent a lot of time talking, catching up on what had happened since I left. I failed to tell them about Sue and the pregnancy, nor that I wanted her to come to St. Cloud where we would be married. They knew that I was married to a woman in San Francisco and had not gotten a divorce yet, something Sue did not know.

I applied for jobs around town but found no work. One place I thought might hire me was the telephone company since my field in the Marine Corps was in communication and radio work. When I applied, I was turned down and told I had too much experience. I was extremely disappointed and floundering. I didn't know what to do or where to turn. Jobs were hard to come by, and I wasn't having any success finding work. Sue was expecting me to send for her, and I couldn't even find a job. I was between a rock and a hard place. I didn't know what the requirements were for getting a divorce and didn't know that there was a waiting period before entering into another marriage. I felt depressed, worthless and inadequate. I would soon be a father and had no concept of the responsibility that went along with that role. I had been dishonest with Sue by not telling her I needed to get a divorce before we could get married. I had been dishonest with the Van Vickles by not telling them about Sue and the child we were expecting. My dishonesty was beginning to catch up with me.

Eventually I had to tell Millie and Willard about Sue and her pregnancy. She was beginning to put pressure on me to come to St. Cloud so we could be married because her pregnancy was beginning to be evident. They wondered what happened to Vera, the woman I married in California. I told them I was still married to her and needed to get a divorce. Willard and I talked. He suggested that I seek legal counsel. I made an appointment with a local attorney and met with him regarding the circumstances of the marriage and the reason for seeking a divorce. I explained that I hadn't seen this woman for over a year. As the spouse of a military man she was receiving my allotment checks. The marriage was one of convenience.

The attorney explained it would take some time to get the paperwork done, as the law required that we attempt to find my spouse. He placed ads in local newspapers of her last known address announcing that a request for divorce was being filed by me. After six weeks with no response to the ads, my divorce was granted.

I called Sue to let her know about meeting with the attorney regarding the divorce and that things were not going well with my finding a job. I told her I was hoping that something would break soon and I would be able to send for her. She was anxious to come to Minnesota as the baby inside her was beginning to grow, and her pregnancy was becoming more obvious every day.

I finally found a job shoveling coal. When someone ordered a ton of coal, I would shovel that amount into a truck then drive it over to the customer's house and shovel it into their coal bin. That job paid one dollar an hour. Needless to say, that was not enough to support a wife and child.

Willard had acquired about six trucks by this time and was hauling live cattle to Landy Packing Company in St. Cloud. I talked to him to see if I could possibly go to work for him driving truck. He said, if I got a chauffeur's license, he would hire me. I went to City Hall, got the book and studied for the license. I then applied for the test and passed it. That was the beginning of my truck-driving experience. My learning to drive a truck was a blessing because, when things were bleak for us financially, I could always revert to driving a truck in order to make a living.

While working for Willard, I made between seventy-five and eighty-five dollars a week, and I thought that would be enough for Sue and me to live on. There would not be much excess, but we could afford a roof over our heads, and I could put food on the table. That was a huge relief. I felt elated that I had a job working for Willard, and now the divorce would soon be granted. I could call Sue and tell her to come to St. Cloud, that I thought we could make it on what I was being paid. Little did I know that this was the beginning of the downward spiral of my alcoholism and eventual suicide attempt.

Thirteen

Wedding Bells for John and Sue

Millie, my step-mom, said that Sue and I needed to get married right away. She said that we couldn't be living together without being married, and she really kept pounding that home. I was trying to think of a way for us to get married as quickly as possible when Sue got to St. Cloud but had to wait for the divorce to be final.

In the meantime, I had my work cut out for me. Each time I returned from being on the road with the truck, I'd go out looking for a place we could afford. About a week later, I found a furnished place. I put the deposit down on it and gave them a move-in date. Now I had to get out and take care of necessities like housewares, linens, and food. With Millie's help, I bought the things we thought we needed until Sue could get here to help select the things she wanted. All I had to do now was anxiously await her arrival.

When Sue arrived in St. Cloud, it was a joyous reunion. She was glad to be here and was excited but, at the same time, frightened about what our future would hold. It was hard for her being so far away from her home and family. I continued to assure her of my love for her and that we would make it, no matter what, it eased some of her fears. There was no waiting period for marriage in Iowa after a divorce, so, as soon as my divorce was final, we drove across the border and were married by a justice of the peace on March 8, 1957. Millie and Willard knew we couldn't afford a honeymoon, so when we returned home, they invited some of our friends and had a small surprise party for us. They were always so good to us and always willing to help ease Sue's homesickness and became like a second family to her. After the party, we moved into our apartment. It wasn't very big: a bedroom, living room, and kitchen, but it was a place we could call home.

I felt good that later we were able to be married in the Catholic Church, and I made a vow that the children would be raised Catholic. Regardless of the difficulties in our marriage, that is one promise, with Sue's help, I did fulfill.

Those first months after our marriage was a lonely time for Sue because I would get up about noon to go to work, and most of the time I would have to go to Fargo, North Dakota, pick up a load of cattle and drive back home to St. Cloud to the packing company. Some nights, before going home, I'd have to fuel the truck and drive to South St. Paul, pick up another load of cattle, bring them back to St. Cloud and unload them. I would then take the truck back to the terminal, park it, go home and try to get some sleep. The next day, the same thing would start all over again. I would earn between $85 and $105 a week, depending on how many loads I took. It was a lot of hard work, but at least it provided us with enough money for the necessities.

As I looked at the impact of a child on our lives and what I was going to do to support that child, I was terrified. I could barely remember my childhood and had no role model in my background whose knowledge I could draw on to know how to raise a child. However, we did start making plans, which included a list of things needed for the arrival of a baby. I handled my insecurity by drinking every chance I got. When we went to St. Paul and had to wait for a load of cattle, other drivers and I would go across the street to a bar and drink beer. Willard never said anything because he was drinking heavily himself. Whenever he could come up with an excuse, he would go with us, and we would drink until we left for home. He always rode with me, and one of the first stops as we left St. Cloud would be the liquor store. Little did I know back then that I was on my way to becoming an alcoholic.

Millie became like a mother to Sue as she accepted and befriended her. Millie is only eleven years older than Sue, and they became very close. Sue was able to confide her hopes, dreams, fears, disappointments, and joys to Millie. They shopped for the baby and found many things at garage sales. By the time the baby arrived, we were pretty well set.

Another thing that worried me a lot was that we had absolutely no insurance and didn't know how we were we going to pay for delivery of a baby. The pressures were really building, and I started to drink more and more. It seemed that when I had any time off, the first thing I would think about was going to have a few beers. The few would always end up being more like a half a dozen or so. At first Sue tried to join in, but it wasn't any fun for her because she just didn't drink that much and didn't care to go into the bars and just hang out. My response to that was that I would stay out on my own and get home later and later; this made life that much more lonesome for her.

FOURTEEN

Baby Girls Join the Family

The baby was due around March 15. The date came and went and no baby. After a week and a half past the due date, Sue went into labor, but it was false labor. We went to the hospital, but after a few hours she was sent home. We went out dancing the next Saturday night, and during the night her water broke, and off to the hospital we went. On April 2, 1957, our first daughter, Sharon Kay, was born. She was the most beautiful child we had ever seen. She had dark curly hair and lots of it, just like mine. Her complexion was dark, and everyone said she looked just like me. We were proud parents and just marveled at how beautiful Sharon was and how much we loved her. Because we had no hospital insurance, Sue stayed in the hospital only one night and went home to Millie's at discharge so I could return to work. Millie helped Sue as her own mother would have done had she been around. I did talk to St. Cloud Hospital and made arrangements to be put on a payment schedule to pay the hospital bill. We just didn't have the money to pay for it all at once.

99

I hated having to leave Sue and the baby, but I had to go back to work, and in those days there was no such thing as paternal leave. I continued the run to Fargo every night, and two or three nights a week, I'd go to St. Paul in addition to Fargo. But our life at home wasn't getting better. Soon it became evident that it was harder and harder to make ends meet. I was worried and didn't know what I was going to do. After a few months, Sue found a job at the telephone company. That lightened the financial load as she was also bringing home an income. We had a friend with whom we left Sharon while Sue was at work. With both incomes, the pressure was off for a while.

Sue came from a Catholic background and wouldn't think of using any kind of birth control. After about three months, we found out that she was pregnant again. This meant that fifteen months after our first child, we would be blessed with another. Neither of us had much faith in God at that time. We were both scared because we were having a hard enough time making ends meet, and now we were going to have another child. We would eventually lose Sue's income and again would barely make ends meet. I just didn't know how we were going to manage to raise two children with both of us needing to work just to get enough money together to be able to support the one child.

One thing I did know was that if I drank for a short period of time, it would relieve me of the pressure and I could be happy-go-lucky and not worry about what was going to happen tomorrow or next month or any other point in the future, for that matter. I could forget my troubles, relax and have a good time. The more I drank, the more my marriage began to suffer. I was gone a lot, and Sue was left with the baby and another on the way. She became very unhappy and we started arguing a lot.

Even though I was supposedly an adult, I would still relive some of my childhood days and yearn to see my mother again and wonder what had happened to her. One thing I did learn was that I was very insecure and had an inferiority complex. I covered it up with a superior attitude.

Talk about any subject, I could give my expert opinion, which really revealed my grandiosity and, in addition, self-centeredness. I had a need to be right and was a perfectionist. Add alcohol to that, and I had achieved a lethal combination. What I perceived as the rejection by my parents when I was a boy made a lasting impression on my life. Somehow or another, I must have interpreted being sent away as not living up to expectations. I felt abandoned even though I knew that was not what had happened.

Sue and I wanted to live closer to the Van Vickles. On Grandpa and Grandma's property there was a little one-room house with a stove, refrigerator, table and chairs and some cupboard space, which we could use as a kitchen. There was a garage across the alley that could be converted into a large bedroom and an outdoor toilet. We went to work and converted the garage and moved in. Yes, we had to go outside to get from the kitchen to the garage and bathroom. It certainly wasn't what most people would accept today, but the set-up worked pretty well at the time. It was spring when we moved in; however, winter would have been a real problem had we continued to live there.

By this time, Millie and Willard had two children. Rocky, the youngest was about two years old, and Randy was about four or five. Rocky was visiting us one day. Sue was very pregnant and was cooking. As she reached over the stove, her smock caught on fire, and she screamed and ripped it off. It scared poor Rocky so badly, he took off running for home. Of course, Millie and Grandma and Grandpa came running to make sure things were okay. Sue was very lucky. Her quick thinking paid off as she only suffered a first degree burn on her arm. God was watching over us, for sure. It could have been so much worse.

Shortly after that incident, on July 16, 1958, our second child was born. It was another beautiful baby girl. We took her

Willard, Millie, and their sons, Randy (standing) and Rocky.

home from the hospital without a name because we couldn't agree on one. I wanted to name her Karen Shay, but Sue thought that would be too close to Sharon Kay. Eventually I won out.

Karen also had lots of black hair that came down over her ears. (No wonder Sue had such heartburn.) She had dark skin and little puffy cheeks and was so cute. Even though it was a happy occasion, adding new responsibilities to my life was a frightful experience. I was anxious about fatherhood and being able to support my family.

Sue and I had talked about our life. It seemed that with the way I was working, we spent very little time together, could barely make ends meet and certainly weren't able to save anything, so we decided that we would move to Richmond, Virginia, Sue's hometown. We thought that Sue would not be as lonely if she were around her family, and I thought I could get a job there and make a better living for us. Millie, Willard, and Grandma and Grandpa were wonderful to us, but it wasn't the same for Sue as being around her own family. All of her biological and extended family lived in Richmond, and she missed them terribly. She was very homesick, and I was gone so much. She thought being closer to her family would make the situation better. Eight days after Karen was born, we decided to leave for Virginia. After saying our goodbyes to Grandma and Grandpa Van Vickle and Willard and Millie and their two boys, Rocky and Randy, we loaded all of our belongings into the car, and with the two children, headed for Richmond.

It took us about a day and a half to get to Richmond. When we got there, Sue's mom invited us to stay at her place until I could find a job. We took her up on her generous offer, and I started looking for work.

PART TWO

Downward Spiral into Alcohol Addiction and Subsequent Recovery

Part two can be looked upon as a teaching tool about the disease of alcoholism. The reader learns that alcoholism is a disease that affects the entire family. Very often, alcoholics are looked upon as people who could really control their drinking and are just weak-willed. Others feel sorry for the family and wonder why the spouse puts up with the alcoholic's behavior. Little do they know that as the family adjusts to the alcoholism, members take on different roles of enabling the alcoholic behavior, thus keeping the alcoholic from seeking needed help.

Chapters fifteen to thirty-two are true "teaching chapters." The inquiring reader will find much information about the disease of alcoholism, signs of it, and treatment centers where those driven to alcohol can get the help they need to live at peace with their families.

FIFTEEN

Job Losses and Alcoholism

I found an ad for a truck-driving job hauling cattle. I knew that's not what I wanted to do permanently, but I had experience in that. I felt I could make a living driving until I could find something else more suitable to meet our needs. It was hard work. I was gone a lot at night, just like before, and I had to sleep during the day. The job did pay fairly well but it was still not quite enough to support the family and get a place of our own. I kept checking the ads for something better while I continued my driving job. It took somewhere between three and six months before I saw an ad for a job at the paper mill.

I applied there, but I had no idea what to expect. I was hired and started at the lowest position possible. The official name of the position I was given was Broke Boy. Huge cylinders rotated the wet paper that was draped over the hot rollers to dry. The rollers were about six feet tall, and the paper dried as it passed over them. Once in awhile the paper would break and drop down under the steam rollers into a pit which was about four feet deep. The steam would come off the huge drums and collect in the pit. When the paper would break, we would have to climb down there, tear the paper into chunks we could handle and throw it out onto the floor. Then a crew would pick it up to be recycled. It was about 110 degrees down in the pit, and all any of us could stand at one time would be about fifteen minutes. I believe that was the hardest of all the work I had ever done in my life. I lasted about three months; I just couldn't see myself doing that for the rest of my life, so I quit.

Up until that time since the move, I had controlled my drinking fairly well. Sue's mom was the deterrent. I knew she would not tolerate my showing up drunk at her home.

I kept watching the ads, putting in applications for work. When I saw that Reynolds Metals Company had an opening, I applied, was called in for an interview and was hired within a week. Reynolds Metals was starting a new department where they were going to be developing coils for automobiles. They were hiring people for a new assembly line, and three of us were hired as quality control people. It was going to be our responsibility to test the coils as they came off the assembly line to make certain that they met specifications. It sounded as if it was going to be an interesting job. I was hopeful that this was the break I had been looking for, working for a company with a decent salary and benefits. Technology at that time was beginning to develop quite rapidly. After working there about six months, the automobile makers had found a different way to get the sound out of a horn, and they weren't going to need the coils that we had been in the process of developing. That essentially closed that project, and all of us were without jobs.

I was disappointed. I had looked forward to the possibility of advancing with Reynolds Metals Company as it was a good company and I felt I could make a career there. Once again I felt lost, wondering what I was going to do next to make a living. I started drinking on a regular basis, telling Sue I was out looking for work while spending a lot of time in bars drinking.

Sue also began looking for work as we realized one of us had to be working, and I was unable to find a job that would support us. We realized we were not going to be able to make it on one income. As we made plans for Sue to go to work, we knew we would need a babysitter for the two girls. There was a woman who lived down the street from Sue's mom and was babysitting two or three other children. Everyone called her Nanny. Sue found a job at Retreat Hospital where she had worked while still in high school. They were very glad to hire her back as she already had experience working in the business office. They knew she was dependable and a good worker.

I still hadn't found a job and felt terrible. Sue was able to do what I should have been doing, provide for the family. I was desperate for work and that prompted me to talk to Sue's uncle, who owned an office supply company called Virginia Impressions Products Company (VIPCO). He agreed to hire me and gave me a job as manager of the warehouse. It was an office supply business that her uncle started in his home, selling typewriter ribbons and supplies. The business had grown rapidly to a full-fledged office-supply company. I was responsible for the overall operation of the warehouse and for the incoming merchandise. It was a good job.

Those were some pretty good times. Sharon and Karen were beautiful children, and they were such happy kids, or so we thought. Not until many years later, when they were adults, did they ever share with us that Nanny would make them sit either in the high chair or by her side all day while she watched TV and, if they misbehaved, she would pull their hair.

On Saturdays Sue's uncle expected all the employees to be at a meeting at the company site to evaluate how the past week had gone. He started the meeting by bringing out a bottle of bourbon, and everyone would start drinking and talking about their accomplishments and achievements during the course of the week. Around one or two o'clock in the afternoon, the meeting would end and we would go home. It was at one of these meet-ings that I asked my boss if I could try to sell some office equip-ment. He told me to go ahead and try. I was excited. I went out on a Saturday and sold a mimeograph machine and wrote up a couple orders for some paper and ink and other various sup-plies. My boss decided that he would put me on as a salesman and hired someone else for the warehouse. After training the new warehouse person, I started in sales.

I was earning $100 a week, but I had to pay my expenses out of that. After about six months, I went to my boss and told him that I couldn't support the family on the salary he was pay-ing me, and he agreed. He said he knew it was tough in Richmond because he had six other salesmen in the area. Therefore, the accounts in the metro and surrounding areas were pretty well saturated by those people. He asked me if I would go to Newport News, Virginia, and take over that area. After discussing the move with Sue, we agreed that we would do it. We went down to Newport News and were fortunate enough to be able to buy a home and began settling in.

I started to work my new sales area, and Sue stayed home with the girls who were about three and four years old. Newport News was not a big city. It had only one large business, the Newport News Shipbuilding and Dry Dock. The vice president of VIPCO already had that account, and no one else could work it. I struggled trying to open new accounts and meet my sales quota.

After three or four months, the president of VIPCO came down to work with me to try and help me establish some new accounts. We went out and worked together. After pounding the pavement all day, he had not sold a single thing nor did he estab-lish any new accounts. At least I felt vindicated. If the profes-sional had come and couldn't sell anything either, he certainly couldn't blame me for not being able to meet the sales quota. I did know that I could not continue to try to make it on $100 a week and pay my own expenses.

There was a real estate office in Newport News, and the owner was a customer of mine. He thought I had a great sales personality and had been after me to go to work for him selling real estate for quite some time. I decided I would give it a try. I studied for and passed the real estate exam after about a month and went to work selling real estate. That didn't last long either. I could draw $100 a week, but houses weren't selling that fast. I didn't have a single sale after three months.

Our bills were beginning to pile up. Sue had just found out she was pregnant again and stayed upset most of the time with my drinking and our money problems. I could always find money to drink but had trouble paying the bills. It was a good thing we lived out of town as Sue was able to hide the problems from her mother and sister. Her brothers were too young to care about anything that went on at that time.

The president of VIPCO told me about an opening becoming available at Speed O Print out of Chicago. They were manufacturers of duplicating equipment and supplies, and he suggested I give them a call. After talking to Sue, I decided to see what it entailed. When I told them I had worked for VIPCO, they offered me the job over the phone. I would be the factory representative for the State of Iowa. The company would pay me $125 a week, and out of that I would pay my own expenses. It would mean that I'd have to move my family to Fort Dodge, Iowa. They would pay my expenses to Chicago for three days of training prior to the move. Bills were beginning to pile up in Newport News, and I thought a geographical change would give us a new beginning. I was unaware at that time that, no matter where I moved, I always had to take me along. Once again I was developing a pattern with a predictable outcome of a downward spiral into alcoholism.

Once I got the family moved and settled in Fort Dodge, I began my new venture. I would leave home in the morning and go from town to town, contacting office supply dealers, introducing myself as their new representative from the Speed O Print Company and sell them stencils, copy machines, or duplicating machines. It was a lot of driving and a lot of wear and tear on an automobile. Expenses came out of the $125, and I could see the handwriting on the wall. I was not going to be able to make it. By now I had tried several different jobs, and nothing had panned out.

I felt like a failure. I started drinking every day. I would go to the VFW and play cards for money, drink and spend less and less time at home. I was ready to give up. I was not able to support the family, no matter what I tried. I knew it was just a matter of time before the company was going to fire me because I was not producing.

It was 1961, and Sue and I had two children and another on the way, and I just couldn't seem to get it together. We were living in Iowa, I wasn't close to anyone I knew in St. Cloud, and Sue was away from her family as well. We were both lonely and growing further apart. Sue was becoming more miserable all the time, and I was dealing with my loneliness and my insecurity by drinking and staying out half the night, many nights not coming in until two, three, or four o'clock in the morning. I hung out at the VFW playing cards, drinking and just ignoring Sue and the kids.

It was about November 1961, with Christmas just around the corner, and I didn't know what I was going to do for the children. I managed to pull together a few dollars and buy a few small presents for them, and Sue had made some things. We went to St. Cloud for Christmas and enjoyed being with the Van Vickles who had presents for all of us.

SIXTEEN

Addiction and the Family

During the week between Christmas and the new year, the realization that things were just going from bad to worse hit me. My drinking, gambling and staying out late continued to be a problem over which I seemed to have no control. On New Year's Eve, I finally told Sue, "Here are the keys to the car." I gave her some money and helped her pack her things in the car saying, "Go to Richmond. Go back to your family."

She didn't want to go, but I forced her into going. I felt totally useless and a failure as a husband and a father. I know I must have wounded her deeply. I forced onto Sue and the children the feelings of rejection, abandonment, loneliness, fear, and all the emotions a traumatic experience like being told to leave invokes in another human being. She and the children deserved much better. And in sending them back to Richmond, I thought they would be better off at home with her mother. I said, "Goodbye," and told Sue to go.

Both our hearts were broken as she started the long drive to Richmond, Virginia, not understanding what had happened or my reasoning in sending her away. She later told me there was a snowstorm in Virginia when she arrived, and her mother was furious with me. Sue defended me by saying, "Mom, I know he's sick," and I was. But neither of us knew how sick I was or the true nature of my illness. During my childhood, I could solve problems by using my wits, but now my wits were too soaked in alcohol and fear to be of any help to me.

I went down to a car lot and bought a used car. A drinking buddy of mine suggested we go to California, and I agreed. I had to go somewhere, anywhere I could make a living, and we took off for California. He was a heavy drinker also, and we drank our way up and down the coast. In the mornings, we looked for a job and by noon we started drinking. We couldn't find anything, and decided to go back to Iowa. I got a job with a guy building chain-link fences. The only catch was that every winter the group with which he worked went to Mexico, and I didn't want to go to Mexico. I asked him if he could refer me to anyone in California who built fences, and he gave me the name of a fence company in Los Angeles. I drove back to Los Angeles and luckily was able to go to work for that company building fences in the Los Angeles area. A lot of times we went to the Beverly Hills Area and put up chain link fences for the celebrities that lived there in the hills.

In March 1962 our third daughter, Cynthia Anne, was born. Sue was living with her mom in Richmond, Virginia. I was in California and wasn't even there for the birth of our child. I had not been in touch with Sue, so she had no way of letting me know about Cindy's birth. She later told me that if I had been anywhere around when she was in labor, she would have killed me. Years later, when I took a good look at my life, I found I had many amends to make and needed the forgiveness of many people, especially Sue, the children and her family.

While in Los Angeles, lonely and alone, I realized how much I missed Sue and the children. I was depressed and lost. I knew our baby was due in March and wondered how my wife and children were. I had to cut down on my drinking as I couldn't afford it and my job entailed physical labor not conducive to a hangover. I had no close associations. I was at my wit's end.

SEVENTEEN

Some Progress, Some Setbacks

In May of 1962, I couldn't stand it any longer and decided to call Sue and see if she would have me back. At first she was very surprised to hear from me. After five months with no contact, she very hesitant to even talk to me. At the same time, she was somewhat hopeful that I had changed and wanted to come back to the family. She was angry at having to go through childbirth alone and felt abandoned and did not encourage me to come home. But she didn't specifically discourage me either.

Sue decided not to say anything to her mother, as she wanted to talk to me in person first. As far as her mom was concerned, I was an irresponsible, good-for-nothing person with whom she would just as soon have no more contact. I really can't say that I blame her, as I think she had every right to feel that way. Even though I was talking to Sue, she kept on being secretive with her mom because she'd made her mom a promise that she would never see me or talk to me again. Sue's mom said that if Sue chose to see me, she would have to move out on her own. Sue also was insecure and fearful of how she would manage raising three children on her own. She needed the security of knowing that she had some support from her family, especially her mom.

After a while, I decided to chance going back to Richmond. It was about the end of May or the first of June. I quit my job in Los Angeles and took what few possessions I had, put them in a bag and started to hitchhike from California to Richmond. There were long periods of waiting as I stood on the highway waiting for a ride. During the day it would get so hot that one could only stand it for a little while and then have to go inside for shade or air conditioning in order to cope with the heat. I stayed in a motel a couple of nights. Five days later I arrived in Richmond.

I called Sue. We talked and arranged to meet without her mother's knowledge. She brought Cindy with her for our first meeting. Cindy was another beautiful daughter. This meeting was the beginning of a downward spiral for Sue as well, as now she was beginning to be caught up in her own behaviors of lying to protect me and defending me by excusing my behavior. We continued to meet without her mother's knowledge. I was staying away from alcohol, and Sue was beginning to believe we could make it together.

We didn't feel good about the secrecy, but Sue was fearful that, if her mother knew she was seeing me, she would have to move out. Sue knew her weakness, where I was concerned, and knew that if she had to move out, it would only be a matter of time and we would be back together again. She knew my biggest problems were my inability to maintain a job that would support a family and support my insatiable drinking habit at the same time. She wanted to wait awhile to make sure that I had quit drinking and that I had a steady, decent-paying job. I made all kinds of promises, not knowing if I could keep any of them. I told her I would not drink if she would agree for us to get together and that I would prove to her how much I loved her and the kids.

One afternoon, after we had been together, Sue went back home, and her mother confronted her with the fact that she had been sneaking around and seeing me behind her back. Neither of us knew how she found out, but parents always seem to have a way of finding things out. There was an argument between the two of them. Sue yelled at her mother and said she would move, knowing full well that we would be together and she wasn't ready for that, nor was she strong enough to say no to me.

We began looking for an apartment and in a few weeks found one a block away from where she had been living with her mother. We moved in together. Little did either one of us know the sorrow, pain, and fears my alcoholism was yet to bring to our family. For many years to come, Sue would feel guilty about that incident with her mother. At the same time, she felt justified in blaming her mother for putting her out and causing the misery she would come to feel, due to the effects of the family disease of alcoholism which was clearly evident in our lives.

In the fall of 1963, Sue had a steady job working for a chain of theatres in Richmond, Virginia. Sharon, our oldest child, started school that year. One of Sue's friends bought her seven dresses, as we couldn't afford to buy school clothes. We were so grateful and will never forget her generosity. For Sharon, beginning school was a very traumatic experience. She cried every day and cried all day in school. At the end of the week, when Sue went to pick her up, her teacher told her to take her home and make her stay in her room all weekend and she would be glad to come back to school. Now doing that would seem like abuse, but we did what we were told and it did take care of the problem. When Monday came, Sharon willingly went back to school.

Once again, I found myself looking for a job, and the only thing I knew was sales or driving a truck. Sales wasn't very secure because there was no set paycheck. Driving a truck, I was

Sue, John, and the girls, Easter 1964. Left to right: Sharon, Cindy, and Karen.

gone all the time. I realized I just wasn't prepared to enter the work force and find a decent-paying job. I talked to a previous partner who had worked at VIPCO, and he wanted me to come to work for him and sell office supplies. I did that, and after a couple of months I could tell that, once again, it was just not going to work out. Even though I had made all the promises to Sue about not drinking, I started again. I was very depressed and once again didn't know where to turn.

I talked to Sue and told her that I was going to check myself in at the Veterans Administration (VA) Hospital in Richmond for an evaluation and see if they had any recommendations that would help me cope without alcohol. I checked myself in and was seen by a psychiatrist. After the interview the psychiatrist admitted me to a psychiatric ward.

On the next visit, when the psychiatrist came to see me, he wanted to explore my background, and I told him my whole life story, from the beginning up to the present time. I was as truthful as I could be, at the time, with him. He decided to give me some medication and to start me on insulin shock therapy. I later found out that this kind of therapy is quite a dangerous procedure and is no longer being used. I went through the shock treatment sessions.

About once a week, Sue would be asked to come in for a conference. In one of those sessions, Sue talked about how much my drinking was affecting our lives and the lives of our children. She explained how we moved around so many times, how much trouble I had finding and keeping a job, how I would lose my temper and blow up frequently, how my behavior was extremely irresponsible, and how I wasn't the person with whom she first fell in love. The psychiatrist listened intently and finally looked up at her and said, "With a background like his, who wouldn't drink?"

For me, hearing those words from a professional, and psychiatrist at that, a person who was treating me for depression, only justified my behavior, and I took that to mean my drinking was normal and expected. Sue also realized my illness was an emotional one, and it reinforced for her that I was sick and needed help. I stayed there for about two months before I was discharged.

Sue wanted to help me and tried to be more patient, empathetic and understanding. Little did either of us know at the time that she was beginning to enable my drinking and irresponsibility by making excuses for and accepting my behavior. Unknown to her, she was becoming co-dependent herself.

For the next couple of years, I sold hospitalization insurance, and Sue was also working. Between the two of us we were able to make ends meet and make a go of it.

In 1966, I got a telephone call from Millie that Grandma Van Vickle had died. We were shocked and told them we would be there right away. Sue and I loaded up the car and left the kids with Nanny and took off for St. Cloud. We arrived just in time for the funeral, which was scheduled for the following day. We were happy to see everyone, yet very sad because of Grandma's death. She was buried in Eden Valley about thirty-five miles from St. Cloud, an area where both she and Grandpa had grown up and courted. On the way back from the cemetery, Grandpa wanted me to ride with him. Along the way, he pointed out different places and told me memories of his life with Grandma. It was quite touching. I listened as he shared his love for her. I yearned to have the same kind of love for Sue. We drove back to St. Cloud, and Sue and I decided we would stay with Grandpa at his house that night.

The next morning we just hung around and visited with Grandpa and then went across the alley to see Millie and Willard. We had decided we would leave in a couple days as we needed to get back to the children and back to work. We told Grandpa that the day after tomorrow we were going to have to go back home to Richmond. We had lunch, and afterward Grandpa said, "I'm really hurting. Will you get me one of my pain pills and some water?"

I got him a pain pill and a glass of water. He was sitting in the chair in the living room and in a lot of pain. He took the pill and said that he had to lie down. I helped him into the bedroom and, as he lay down on the bed, he said, "Well, Johnny, I'm going to go now."

I said "Where are you going, Grandpa? We're not going to go anywhere."

He said, "Goodbye," and with that he died.

I shouted for Millie and ran to the telephone and called for an ambulance. Millie ran out into the alley waiting for the ambulance and Willard ran inside to Grandpa. By the time the ambulance got there, Grandpa was dead, and they didn't try to revive him.

Saddened, we called Richmond, Virginia, and made arrangements for the children and stayed another four days for Grandpa's funeral. He was buried next to Grandma in Eden Valley. As I think about these events years later, I think the two of them were so close that Grandpa could not imagine continuing life without Grandma. I think he just gave up and asked God to bring him home to be with the love of his life. God rest his soul. They were beautiful, caring people, and I will always be grateful for the love and care they gave to me as a child and until the day they died.

While we were in St. Cloud, I realized how much I missed being there and missed Willard and Millie. I started feeling people out to see about the possibility of returning. I went to Landy Packing Company where I had previously driven a truck and asked Max Landy if I came back to St. Cloud, could I work for him again. He told me anytime I wanted to come back to town, I should come and see him and I would have a job waiting, After having sold insurance in Richmond, I felt certain I could sell it in Minnesota, if need be.

We left for home. On the way back, Sue and I talked about the struggles we had making ends meet. I shared my desire of returning to St. Cloud with her for the first time. On our ride home, we shared many feelings with each other—our joy and sadness about where our lives had been and our unfulfilled dreams of what we wanted to do. We had no plans or goals for the future but knew things had not been good thus far in our marriage, and we weren't getting anywhere financially. We had a few friends in Richmond and enjoyed getting together to play cards with family and friends, but things always seemed strained between Sue's mother and me. That, plus my instability and all the other problems kept our marriage in chaos. I decided it was time for another geographical change where I thought things might be better.

I shared with Sue that I had been told that if I came back to St. Cloud I could have a job driving a truck and told her I would like to go back. The more we talked, the more agreeable she became, and once again we decided that that's what we were going to do. I would go ahead and get the job and a place to live, and then call her and she would come with the kids. Once I arrived in St. Cloud, I went to see Max Landy and he gave me the job he had promised. After a few days I found a place out in the country on a farm, in a trailer for Sue and the kids and me. It was on the property of a friend who worked for Willard. I called Sue and told her to pack up the kids, that I had found a job and a place to live and sent her the money for bus fare.

She would be leaving for Minnesota in a week or so. One day she overhead her mother saying to a neighbor, "Sue will be home in a few months when things don't work out." You know, when you tell someone they can't do something, they usually set out to prove they can. At that point, Sue vowed to herself that she would not go back home to live ever again. She would go home to visit, but not to live.

She packed the three children and herself up and took the bus for the long ride to Minnesota. I met them at the bus station and took them to the place I had rented that was to be our home. We had only the one car, and I needed that for work so she was stuck out in the country with no transportation to get anywhere. A couple of Millie and Willard's friends helped us out by offering us cheap rent on a trailer located on their farm. Alma was a farm girl and did a lot of gardening, canning and baking. Sue was a city girl and had an extremely difficult time adjusting. She finally told me she refused to live so far out in the country without any way to get into town and that we had to find another place to live. I was disappointed that she was unhappy, but we talked to a niece of Willard's, and she and her husband took us in until we could find another place. They had five children of their own, and we were moving in with our three.

The children enjoyed one another. We were cramped, but somehow we made it work and got along great with them. We soon found a small house on the north side of St. Cloud with a kitchen, living room, one small bedroom upstairs and a basement which we made into a bedroom for the kids. The house had only one bathroom which was in the basement. We lived there for a year or so until we were able to find a place on the east side of town that was larger and closer to Willard and Millie and my work. It was owned by a friend who also owned the grocery store where we shopped. We had a credit account at the store, and he knew we would pay our bills on time, so he agreed to let us rent the house.

The house was old but newly remodeled and looked quite nice. We had fun buying furniture and decorating the house. I remember Sue found plastic curtains for the windows, and we did a lot of shopping at garage sales. I was making decent money driving truck, and we were able to buy the girls bicycles that year for Christmas. They were so elated and thrilled, and so were we because we were able to do something special for them. Sue was not working and stayed at home. She was happy being a mom. We had fun during the next few years, partying, going to dances and just being together with family and friends. I had started drinking again, but Sue was also drinking some, and it wasn't that big of a problem for her until my drinking began to increase.

At that time the best paying truck-driving job happened to be at Fingerhut, so, when I had a couple of days off, I went and applied. It only took two or three days for them to call and offer me a job. Their trucks were running steady, and the company was very busy and wanted me to come to work as soon as possible. I quit my job at Landy Packing Company. I thanked Max for helping me out when I needed a job. I told him why I was leaving. He was very nice, and we parted as friends. I knew that if I ever got in a jam again I could always go back to work for him.

When I started driving for Fingerhut, we dispatched to Detroit, Michigan, running double, which meant two drivers in one truck, one sleeping and one driving. It would normally take us three days to make the trip, which made it a short week. My driving partner had a farm and, when we got home, he did not want to go out on the road again because of the farm work. Normally there was another load of goods that had to go to Madison, Wisconsin, so I would take that run by myself. I could do it in about fourteen hours. That run would pay $250 by itself and I would end up making $500 to $600 every week. That was a great income at that time and, for the first time ever, we didn't have our backs against the wall. Even though I had to be gone quite a bit, we felt we were on easy street because we had enough money to pay our bills, and we didn't have to worry about where the next penny was coming from. We were able to buy some furniture that we were lacking—our very first new appliance was a refrigerator. It was a side-by-side refrigerator which we purchased for $500 and later used it to make a down payment on a house.

When I did come home, we partied hard. My drinking was again becoming a problem for Sue. On my days off, I would spend a lot of time over at Willard's station where someone always had a bottle of brandy, and I could always find a case of beer.

My job appeared stable, and I was making good money, so we decided to start looking for a house to buy. We found one in a new housing development called Pleasant Acres in St. Joseph, Minnesota, a few miles west of St. Cloud. I told Sue I didn't know if we could buy that particular house, but it would be fun to go and look at it. That's just what we did. The development owner was present when we arrived and was anxious to show us the home. It was brand new, beautiful and furnished with all the appliances. He said I could qualify for the home, which was priced at $18,500, and he was selling it "Contract for Deed," with a required down payment of $500. I told him I didn't have the $500 cash, but I had just purchased a new side-by-side refrigerator, which was still in the crate, and I asked him to accept that as a down payment. He said he was building more homes in the area and could use it in another home and agreed to accept my offer. I was somewhat concerned because the house payment was $298 a month, and I had only been in that job for six months. If something happened to the job, we were going to be stuck with a house payment that we wouldn't be able to manage. Well, we bought the house anyway and were to close and move in on September 1, 1968. It was an exciting time for all of us as this was the first brand new home we ever purchased.

I went back to work. When I came back off the road, I asked the dispatcher if I could use a truck to move. He gave me permission to do so. I called Willard, and he arranged to have a couple of his drivers help us. Sue had already packed everything and was ready for the move. We loaded the truck, and Sue and the girls followed us in the car as we drove to Pleasant Acres. After eleven years of moving from place to place, we finally had a home we could call our own, and Sue was happy. However, she was concerned about the amount of drinking I was doing again.

As soon as we were unpacked and settled, I had to get back into my uniform and be ready to leave that evening for another trip. That happened to be the busy season, as it was getting close to Christmas. We were running heavy at that time, and I was making good money, but it wasn't easy. Many times we ran double. Our trips would take us across the country and back to St. Cloud with just enough time off to go home, change clothes, say, "Hi" and "Bye" to the family and go back out that same night.

We moved into our house on September 1, 1968, and I didn't sleep in my own bed until December 6, 1968, when I told the dispatcher I was taking a day off. He said I had to take the trip, and I refused, telling him, "I just moved into my new home on September 1, and I haven't spent a single night in my own bed. I plan on doing so tonight because it is my birthday."

He agreed to give me a couple of days off. When I went home it was almost like a reunion. It was great. Sue knew, just as I did, that we had the increased responsibility of house payments along with the children, and, therefore, I had to continue to work hard driving truck to provide for my family and allow Sue to stay at home with the family.

While driving for Fingerhut, the person I was teamed up with was also a heavy drinker. When we would come in from a trip, we would decide which one of us would start out, and the one who started the trip would agree to stay sober. It was like having a sober driver today. We would begin our trip, and the first driver would drive between six and eight hours and then stop at a truck stop to eat, fuel up and switch drivers. We did this all the way to our destination. Once at our destination, we would unload at the postal distribution center, then go on to our next destination and pick up a full load of goods to bring back to Fingerhut in St. Cloud. Fingerhut would sell these items out of their catalogs and distribute them out of St. Cloud to customers throughout the United States.

The Fingerhut drivers were a close-knit group. If we were in town and had a couple of days off, we would meet at a place like O'Hara Brothers' Bar and Grill to socialize and have a few drinks. Our life revolved around working, time off, going out drinking and then back out on the road again.

As my drinking increased, Sue was happier when I was on the road than when I was at home. It seemed as if all we did now was argue when I was at home. In Sue's eyes, the household was much more peaceful with me gone. It felt as if I no longer had any input into their lives, other than financial. She and the girls were making a life without me. Time was passing, and the girls were growing up really fast. Sharon was now eleven, Karen was ten, and Cindy was six years old.

Little did I know that my job with Fingerhut would be coming to an end. I was beginning to burn out being on the road all the time and then coming home and not having any time with the family. I seemed to be drifting further and further apart from the ones I really loved. When I did get time off, I would go out drinking, leaving Sue and the girls alone. Then I was back on the road again. It was really wearing on me and putting a huge strain on our marriage and family life as well. I did not realize that I was progressing deeper and deeper into the depths of my alcoholism.

On one of the trips going out to New York, we were on the way over to pick up some tools. My partner was driving, and, as he started to make a left-hand turn, a truck coming from the right side hit us. I was sitting in the passenger seat. The impact broke the fuel tank and threw me across the cab of the truck into my partner's lap. An ambulance was called. My knee was banged up and bleeding, and my leg was swollen and stiff. I was taken to the local hospital emergency room, and after being treated and having stitches in my knee, I was discharged. We called Fingerhut, and the dispatcher arranged to have me flown home. When I arrived at the airport, my ticket was waiting for me. Upon my arrival in Minneapolis, Sue was waiting to take me home. The knee was injured pretty badly, and it took a while before I could walk on it, let alone sit for hours with it bent in one position. I was drinking again, and decided that I was going to quit driving because I just couldn't take the hours I was putting in.

Once again I found myself in the vicious circle of looking for a job, no money, heavy drinking, arguing at home, neglecting the family and feeling worthless and a failure as a husband and a father. I couldn't hold a job. I didn't have the experience or training to do anything else except possibly sales. My life was a merry-go-round and, as a family, we were becoming more divided and miserable.

Sue was begging me to stop drinking. I would make promises to stop, but I couldn't keep them. That would lead to arguments between us, shouting back and forth and her making threats to take the girls and leave. When I would come home drunk, these scenes would take place in front of the girls. It was not a good situation. I would go out again and get drunk and on the way home knew I had to face Sue again with another broken promise. I was getting ideas in my head that Sue and the kids would really be better off without me. I would start to fantasize about ways to commit suicide. Most of them would involve my crashing the car into something. Most of the times, this would only be in my thoughts as I would think of how easy it would be to take the car and drive it into a telephone pole.

When I was in town, I would go over to see Willard where I knew we would end up drinking. Usually that would be at the garage where he had his trucking business, or we would get in his pickup and go out on a lake somewhere fishing and drinking out there. It seemed that all of the activities in my spare time just revolved around drinking. Sue was constantly nagging me and reacting to my drinking with anger and threats to leave. She complained to the kids and everyone else and tried to have them take sides.

She later discovered that her life had been revolving around me and my drinking just as my life revolved around drinking. It was more powerful than either of us, and I started thinking again of ending it all by committing suicide. I believed Sue and the kids would be better off without me. Little did I know that she was having some of the same thoughts about her own life. We would later discover, as we learned about the disease of alcoholism, how this disease could extend its hold, not only on an individual, but those around them as well.

Today, I realize that many of the friends I had chosen were also alcoholics. One of them committed suicide by backing his truck up to his fish house, left the motor on, took a vacuum cleaner hose and stuck one end over the tail pipe of his pick up, and the other end in his fish house. He went inside, opened a bottle of brandy and the next morning he was found dead from carbon monoxide poisoning. As I would think about his suicide, I'd say to myself, "If I ever get that bad, I'll quit drinking." Little did I know that I was already heading in the direction of suicide every time I got drunk and had thoughts about smashing the car into a telephone pole. I didn't understand that the disease of alcoholism had its hold on me. When I drank, I would lose control, and regardless of the pain it caused those around me and the promises I would make to quit drinking, I couldn't stop without help. Nor could I see that my life had now become unmanageable.

In 1969, things were no better than the previous year. After going on a fishing trip, I did not return home when I said I was going to and got drunk instead. Sue hit bottom and called a counselor whom she had met while visiting a friend in treatment at Willmar State Hospital. He informed her that she couldn't do anything to change me or my drinking, but she could do something about herself and referred her to a program for spouses and family members of someone who was having trouble with alcohol. People went there to learn about alcoholism. They learned about themselves and gained support of others who had experienced similar situations. They obtained the tools necessary to change their own lives. In time, they learn detachment with love.

Sue began going to meetings at least once a week, and I began to see a change in her. I didn't know what that was all about. She would no longer argue with me, fight or beg me to stop drinking. She would just say things like, "If you want to do something about your drinking, you can go to a program that can assist you in gaining sobriety and find out how other people are doing it."

That would just make me more angry. I'd think, "Who is she to tell me what's good for me?"

I was no longer driving a truck and had received some profit sharing money from Fingerhut. I had a background in office supply sales and decided I could start a business in St. Cloud. I rented an office, bought some ribbons, carbon paper duplicating supplies, copy machines and general office supplies and put together an office-machine supply business. As I was the only employee and did not have to answer to anyone but myself, my downward spiral into alcoholism accelerated. I would order some equipment, go out and find a customer, sell a piece of equipment, then take the profits, pay some of our bills at home, and turn around and spend the rest on beer.

Some days, instead of going to work, I would get together with another alcoholic friend of mine at his house at eight o'clock in the morning with the grand idea of going fishing that day. We would leave his house, go buy a six-pack of beer and start drinking. Some days we would go out fishing for about an hour or so but then the rest of the time would be spent either in a bar or riding around from lake to lake drinking as we went. That would go on all day and into the night.

131

I would tell myself that I had to get home for supper, but we would just continue to drink. The next thing I knew, the bar was closing, and I would start home, berating myself and calling myself all kinds of names like, "You dummy, you did it again. Why don't you just go ahead and end it all? Sue and the girls would be better off without you anyway." That went on day after day. There might be a break from this pattern here and there for a day, but it certainly didn't last long, and I would be back doing the same thing again.

EIGHTEEN

Sue's Ultimatum and New Hope

Sue had said that if I wasn't willing to do anything about my drinking, I should not bother to come home. She also told me that she was going to get a divorce. I wanted things to be different, yet I wouldn't admit it to anyone. When I realized Sue was serious about the divorce, I thought I had better do something to stop her from letting that thought continue. I decided I would enter a program designed to help people who had drinking problems and maybe that would be enough to please her. I tried to taper my drinking but was unable to do so.

There was a treatment place called Pioneer House in Medicine Lake, Minnesota. I talked to Sue about going into treatment. She was thrilled. We called, and two days later I entered treatment. I had a friend pick me up and drive me down to Pioneer House.

There were probably about twenty other guys in treatment. Every day, for a week, we would get a vitamin shot because most of us were debilitated from drinking, not eating much and not getting the nutrition we needed. That was one way to help stabilize the patients. It didn't seem like much of a program of recovery. The objective seemed to be to keep us from drinking and introduce us to a life of sobriety. Here was my first real introduction to the Twelve Steps Program. This program, still being used, is a set of guiding principles for recovery from addiction, compulsion, or other behavioral problems. In my case, it was addiction to alcohol. Even though I didn't agree with a lot of what went on in the meetings at Pioneer House, I was exposed to messages delivered on a daily basis.

Step One of the Twelve Steps Program states, "We admitted we were powerless over alcohol, and that our lives had become unmanageable." I had no problem with my life being unmanageable. I thought I could stop drinking anytime I wanted, and I sure wasn't powerless over alcohol.

Step Two states, "Came to believe that a power greater than ourselves could restore us to sanity." I didn't agree with that one at all because I sure wasn't insane. Little did I know that I was setting myself and my family up for a lot more heartache and pain. The insanity of the illness was that I believed I was sane while the people who loved me lived with the insanity on a daily basis. The disassociation from church and from the God of my understanding led me into spiritual bankruptcy. That allowed the thoughts of suicide and the insane thoughts of "The family would be better off without me" to ferment and grow.

Sue came to visit one time while I was in treatment, and before long, I was back home.

I had all these grand ideas about what I was going to do and how I was going to make it up to Sue and the girls. For about three months, I didn't drink at all, although I thought about drinking a lot. I eventually said to myself, "I have the knowledge of what not to do and surely a couple of drinks won't hurt."

With that in mind, I would go out and experiment. I found I could stop drinking after having one or two bottles of beer and/or liquor. I repeated this pattern for a short period of time, which only helped to convince me I was not an alcoholic. Before long, however, I found myself right back where I left off, drinking all day and all night.

I was depressed again. Sue was deeply hurt, angry and felt betrayed and lied to. The children were probably ashamed because their friends would see me drunk when I came home. I was again caught in my insane behavior where alcohol was more important than my existence. Sue continued going to meetings with spouses of alcoholics. More and more, she understood that the disease of alcoholism was truly at work in me.

In the summer of 1970, Sue's mother and sister came to visit us. Sue had arranged to take them, along with our girls up to the lake in Alexandria, Minnesota, where we had a converted school bus parked on a friend's property. The bus was orange and black, striped like a tiger and had six bunk beds and a table. It was our camper.

When Sue's mom and sister arrived, they took the girls and left for the lake. I had a copy machine to show a prospective customer in Brainerd. I would follow later that day bringing our oldest daughter with me. After everyone had left for the lake, I took the copy machine and started for Brainerd. I got there and made my contact with the person, demonstrated the machine and found they weren't interested. I was dejected over not making the sale, so the way to handle that was to stop by the VFW and have a couple of beers. I told myself I would just have a couple and then get back to St. Cloud, change clothes, pick up our daughter and go meet the family. Well, as usual I got in there to have a couple, and before I knew it, it was afternoon and I told myself I better get going, that the family was expecting me and here I was at the VFW drinking. On the way out of Brainerd, I remember having the thought of, "Oh, you dummy, you did it again."

As I looked ahead, I saw a truck pulled off to the side of the highway. As I got close to the truck, I didn't have another thought. I just jerked the steering wheel, and that's the last thing I remember before I passed out.

My next memory was opening my eyes and being in excruciating pain. I heard someone say, "We better get him out of there before the car starts on fire."

My response was, "That would not be a bad idea."

The rescue people thought I was dead. They got me out of the car and into an ambulance, then transported me to the hospital in Brainerd. Upon my arrival, the doctors examined me, decided they didn't have the facility to treat me adequately, put me back in the ambulance and transported me to the St. Cloud Hospital. When I got to St. Cloud, I discovered I was severely injured with a broken pelvis.

While in the emergency room, I was put in traction and then transferred to a medical floor. I was concerned that Sue and the kids would be wondering what happened to me. I later found out that the sheriff had gone to the house and told our daughter (scared her to death) that I had had a serious accident. She told him where to find Sue. Sue and the gang were out on the lake fishing. A water patrol came out and informed them of my accident. Sue left the children with a friend up at the lake and rushed back to St. Cloud with her mother and sister.

When Sue came to see me, her eyes, her face, her tears told me about everything that I needed to know. She was in so much pain and in such emotional turmoil, all because of me and my selfish, self-centered behavior. I vowed to make it up to her when I got better. I remember I was in a lot of pain, immobile, and believed I was on the verge of dying. I remember closing my eyes for a little bit, and when I opened them again, Sue was sitting there with tears running down her face.

Right at that moment, while lying in the bed with Sue sitting in the chair crying, I saw myself floating toward the window, and then I found myself down on the street. It was dark. It seemed that it was raining and the wind was blowing. There was a bright light in the distance that seemed to be pulling me toward it. All of a sudden I was talking to someone. Not verbally expressing myself, I was talking but it was all in my mind. I was hearing the words coming to me, and I was answering back. Then I saw the light again, a bright light off in the distance, and it was drawing me toward it. Then the voice was giving me a choice, asking if I wanted to continue. I responded by saying "No, not yet, they still need me."

As soon as I said that, I opened my eyes. I was back in bed looking at Sue.

I know without a doubt that there is a wonderful place waiting for us when we pass on. Since that out-of-body experience, I no longer fear death and know I will be at peace.

Sue had a spiritual experience as well. She later told me that she had gone to church in St. Joseph that evening and prayed. As she knelt at the foot of the altar, her prayer went something like this: "Lord, I love John and don't want to see him die, but I do know he suffers from the disease of alcoholism and struggles with it constantly. If it is your will that he recover from that disease, please let him live. However, if he is going to continue to suffer from the disease, I'm ready to release him to your care." She said that when I lived, even though I suffered a while longer with that disease, she knew that someday I would find recovery and stop drinking. During the tough times, she would remember that night when God chose to let me live. Her faith continued to carry her through.

The next day a consulting physician discovered that I had a collapsed lung. I credit him with saving my life. He ran out of the room and initiated orders STAT. Before I knew what was happening, nurses and doctors were all around. An orthopedic physician visited me. He told me I had a broken pelvis. He wasn't sure what they were going to do about it, but he informed me I would be in traction for quite some time. I let him know that I didn't have any medical insurance and asked if I could be transferred to the VA Hospital because I was a veteran and eligible for care there. He said he would see what he could do.

The orthopedic physician made all the arrangements so the Veterans Administration Hospital in Minneapolis would be expecting me the next day. He arranged with a local ambulance company to transport me, and the owner of the company was there to pick me up early the next morning. The owner was a generous person and never sent me a bill. We became good friends. Later, after I recovered, he would invite me to his house to play cards.

I stayed in traction for weeks in Minneapolis. The doctors started discussing what they wanted to do. The consensus was that they wanted to fuse my leg at the hip which would severely limit my mobility. I let them know that I wanted a second opinion and was discharged back home.

I could get around on crutches, and I decided to see an orthopedic surgeon in St. Cloud. I made an appointment and told the surgeon what the doctors at the VA had said about fusion. After numerous X-rays, I asked him his opinion. He suggested that we do a cup orthoplasty. If successful, we had a chance to make me mobile rather than going through the hip fusion. I talked to Sue and together we decided that I would agree to the cup orthoplasty and scheduled the surgery.

In the meantime, since I knew it was going to be a long recovery period, I went down to the Social Security office and filed for Social Security Disability. While I was in the hospital, Sue had seen the veterans service officer and obtained emergency temporary assistance since she wasn't working at the time of the accident.

In 1971, alcoholism had been established as an illness, and insurance companies were beginning to pay for alcohol and chemical addiction treatment. Alcohol and chemical dependency programs were being established throughout the state. Sue continued going to a program for the spouses of alcoholics. She heard of a program for alcoholics starting at the St. Cloud Hospital and knew she wanted to work there. She had started working on an Extended Care Unit and, when the Alcohol and Chemical Dependency (A & C) Unit opened, she asked to be transferred there and was given the position of secretary to the director for the unit. She was able to obtain family insurance through the hospital. This enabled me to go ahead and have the surgery without going further into debt. I agreed to the surgery, and Dr. Jerry Iverson did the procedure. I was in the hospital about two weeks and was then discharged, walking with crutches.

I thought I would be able to discard the crutches in a short period of time, but, much to our disappointment, it did not turn out that way. Whenever I tried to walk, I was in excruciating pain, and the hip joint was extremely painful. Even with the aid of the crutches, it was very difficult to get around. The surgeon had put me on pain medication which helped some, but the problem with that was that it also helped lead me back to drinking. I found that if I took a pain pill and had a couple of drinks on top of that, it would better help me tolerate the pain. Stopping at a couple of drinks was a fantasy, as I was never able to stop at a couple. I just continued to drink. In spite of all my promises and all my good intentions, I was right back where I started, once again. I found myself standing in front of the mirror in the morning and hating the sight of the person looking back at me.

Unknown to me, Sue had filed a petition for commitment for alcohol addiction and suicidal tendencies. One morning, when she was at work, the door bell rang, and there was a sheriff at the front door. He told me to get dressed, that I was being transported to the VA Hospital. The VA Hospital in St. Cloud had also started a chemical dependency unit to treat alcohol and chemical addiction. I happened to be one of their first clients.

When I got to the hospital, I was evaluated, this time by a psychiatrist. He decided to treat me with a variety of medications. By the time I finished taking the medications, I felt worse than I ever did drinking. After being there two weeks, I got a pass to go home for Thanksgiving. Sue picked me up and took me home.

I felt like I was jumping out of my skin all day and asked Sue to take me back to the hospital early. I couldn't stand it at home. Sue wrote down the medications they were giving me and looked them up in the *Physician's Desk Reference* at work. The drugs the psychiatrist was giving me were powerful, and my body was just not tolerating them well. Instead of treating me for alcoholism, the treatment was more psychiatric. After thirty days, I was discharged from the VA and sent back home.

Throughout this ordeal with my alcoholism, the children were being affected. Our children were having difficulties in their relationships with one another and were continually fighting amongst themselves. The oldest, Sharon, was having comprehension problems in school. She was also beginning to take on the parenting role with the other two. Sue would get calls at work from Sharon when the fighting got out of control. She worked with the girls and encouraged them to enroll in a program for children of alcoholics.

It wasn't long after treatment at the VA Hospital in 1971 that I started drinking again. I sincerely started making attempts to stop. I was going to meetings designed for people addicted to alcohol and would hang out there because I was afraid that, if I went out and ran around with my old friends, I would end up drinking again. Many times during these early treatment efforts, I would stop at the liquor store and have a couple of drinks and then go to the meeting place and hang out there because I didn't want to go home. As long as I called Sue from the meeting place, she would be okay and believed I was really trying to stay sober. Family chaos continued.

I tried crazy things, different methods to prove to myself that I was not an alcoholic. For example, I'd stop at the Ace Bar, have one drink and then go home. I continued doing that for a week. I convinced myself that I was not an alcoholic and proceeded to get drunk. That's the insanity of the illness. When not drinking, I would go to St. Cloud Hospital to their chemical dependency unit and volunteer. But when I started drinking again, Sue just gave me an ultimatum: either the bottle or the family. This time she said it with such surety that I knew she meant it and would carry through with a divorce. I knew the games were up and decided that, if I wanted my family, I would have to make it in sobriety. I decided to give sobriety a sincere effort because I loved my family and didn't want to lose them.

I started to volunteer seriously at the hospital. I also went back to my surgeon and told him that what we were doing was not helping and that I couldn't stay on pain medication forever. It wasn't getting any better. I asked, "If you had what I've got, what would you do?"

He said, "I would go to the Mayo Clinic in Rochester and have a total hip replacement." He explained that, even though he could do the surgery himself, the St. Cloud Hospital did not have the isolation techniques at that time to do the necessary total hip replacement. I agreed to go to Mayo, and an appointment was set for me to go to Rochester. After being evaluated at the clinic, a date was set for my surgery. Sue drove me down and stayed with me, and the surgery turned out fine, even though it was very painful. They had me out of bed after two days, into physical therapy and walking on my leg. After seven days, I was discharged with a prescription for pain medication. Sue came to get me and take me home. I was given a pain pill just before we left Rochester. On the outskirts of Rochester, Sue suddenly developed a high fever and chills. I slid over into the driver's seat and drove to St. Cloud, where we stopped at the drug store. Sue ran in and got my prescription filled, and we headed home.

Within about a week, the pain from my leg disappeared. I didn't need the crutches anymore and started walking almost normally. I had only a slight limp. The right leg wound up just a little bit shorter than the left one, but there was no pain. I diligently did the exercises until there wasn't a problem anymore. It took about a month, and I was almost back to normal from the surgery. I continued to meet with others who were trying to stay sober on a regular basis and spent a lot of time at the club socializing and playing cards with the guys. Sue and I began individual counseling. Later we went to counseling as a couple and finally took the children for family counseling to help us cope with the many years of addiction we had experienced.

With the help of counseling, as a family we started making progress in recovery. I think the kids started feeling better about themselves as well. One of our children was still having some problems. We seemed to be going to school every now and then to address some of her behavior. Sue and I came to the conclusion that she had to be drinking alcohol or using marijuana. Of course, she denied that, but we had our suspicions.

Even so, the family seemed to be getting better. Sue started feeling better about our relationship, and I was feeling better about the way the family was getting along. It seemed that all of us were gaining something. We started to go camping on weekends, sleeping out under the stars, sitting around a camp fire in the evening roasting marshmallows and enjoying each other's company. I thought to myself, "Sobriety isn't that hard." The kids loved to play on and in the water. If we caught fish, we would clean them and fry them right after catching them. Life was good.

Nineteen

A Path to Sobriety

One day in 1973, without any planning and without much thought, I wound up drinking again. I drank on into the night and gave a guy with whom I had been drinking a ride over to Sartell. It was about two or three o'clock in the morning. After dropping him off, I realized what I had done. I was filled with remorse, depressed, and as I drove over to the dam I pointed the car over the hill facing the river and just sat there. I thought, "After all this work, progress, and healing, I rip it all apart by drinking and putting the family through this pain again. Maybe I should just end it all and drive the car over the cliff." Then I thought about what God wanted from me, and I remembered the out-of-body experience and of my response, "No, not yet. They still need me."

I seemed to be unable to get my act together and do what was required of me. Once again, I decided they still needed me. I decided to go back to treatment and find out what I had missed the other times. I gave Sue time to get to work at the St. Cloud Hospital, and at eight o'clock in the morning I called her. She suggested that I talk to the program director of the A and C unit.

Even though Sue worked there, the director agreed to let me come into treatment, so I checked myself in and once again started treatment. I was determined I was going to do whatever it took to find what I had missed up to this time. I vowed that I would never put my family through this kind of hell again. I also knew that in order to be able to do what I needed to do, I would have to discover what was wrong with me.

Back in those days, the length of time in the treatment program was ninety days. I knew that it was a long time and yet I thought that because of my having been through two other treatment programs, the staff certainly would not keep me there for ninety days. I was soon to discover that I had a great awakening coming. I learned that I was not privileged. When I thought I was finished with the program, I would find out that I hadn't even started yet. I started to take a serious look at the tools for recovery, the Twelve Steps Program.

Step I: We admitted we were powerless over alcohol, that our lives had become unmanageable. There was no problem with the unmanageability part. I could tell my life had become unmanageable, but I had some problems about being powerless. Yet when I looked at who I was, I had to admit that if I was not powerless, how come I was in treatment for the third time? When I was sober and supposedly in full control, I would start drinking again. Powerlessness? Unmanageability? I continued to use the drug of my choice after numerous promises not to. If that was not powerlessness, then what was? To help me understand the extent of my powerlessness and unmanageability, I received an assignment to write down and share in the group twenty examples of my powerlessness and twenty examples of my unmanageability. Wow, what an eye-opening and humbling experience.

Step II: Came to believe that a power greater than ourselves could restore us to sanity. I certainly didn't have any problem with that step. When I looked back at my behavior, I had to admit that no sane person would do the things that I had done.

Step III: Made a decision to turn our lives and our will over to the care of God as we understood him. Therein lay a lot of my problems. I had no problem calling on God to help me out of a mess. I had no problem asking God why he allowed certain things to happen to me, and I had no problem thanking God for some of the things that he helped me with. But I had never turned my will and my life over to the care of God. Many years later, I learned that it was a good thing that I was feeling guilty. Had it not been for the guilt feelings, I never would have found God and made my peace with him, nor would I have ever found sobriety.

Step IV: Made a searching and fearless moral inventory of ourselves. That meant taking an inventory of my life to discover the bad things I had done and writing them down. It also meant discovering the good things about myself and writing them down as well. As one might suspect, I had no problem going on and on about how bad I was and, when it came to balancing that with what was good, I could find very little on the positive side. That's where I spent a lot of time soul searching. One of the great things I discovered—which might have little meaning to most others but had a lot of meaning to me—was that I was a human being, and, being human, I didn't have to be perfect. All I had to do was be human, go through life, learn from my mistakes, make amends to people I had harmed, and not harm them in the future. If I did, I needed to make amends to them again, admit the mistake, apologize and resolve not to repeat the offense.

Step V: Admitted to God, to ourselves, and to another human being the exact nature of our wrongs. Having gone through the first four steps, it was now time for me to make an appointment with a clergy person, sit down and share the good and bad things about myself.

Step VI: Were entirely ready to have God remove all of these defects of character. Having completed the first five steps, I was ready for Step VI.

Step VII: Humbly ask Him to remove our shortcomings. To me that meant going to church, going to Mass, receiving Communion, and accepting that God created me and loved me in spite of my short comings. Had he wanted me to be perfect, he easily could have made me perfect, but he didn't. He made me the way I was, gave me freedom of choice and let me go out and experience life. He let me take whatever path I wanted, and when the time came and I was ready to accept his forgiveness and return to his loving arms, God was there waiting.

Step VIII: Made a list of all persons we had harmed and became willing to make amends to them all. As I looked back on my life, I needed to write down the names of the people I had harmed: myself, my wife, my children, my extended family, and my friends all had to be on the list.

Step IX: Made direct amends to such people wherever possible, except when to do so would injure them or others. That meant going to the people I had harmed, apologizing and asking their forgiveness.

Step X: Continued to take personal inventory, and when we were wrong, promptly admitted it. I needed to look over the day to see if I'd harmed anyone, if I was cross with anyone, and if I was, at the next opportunity I needed to promptly admit my mistakes and go on.

Step XI: Sought through prayer and meditation to improve our conscious contact with God as we understood Him, praying only for the knowledge of His will for us and the power to carry that out. This meant daily quiet time, prayer, and meditation, seeking God's guidance in my life.

Step XII: Having had a spiritual awakening as the result of these steps, we tried to carry this message to alcoholics, and to

practice these principles in all our our affairs. This is one of my favorite steps. Does that mean that I became this person upon release from treatment? Absolutely not! But those are the steps put before me, steps for me to work on daily, to continue to grow, and in God's good time for him to reveal his plan for me. I can honestly say that when I left treatment this time in 1973, I felt fully liberated from the disease of alcoholism. I had a way, a path to follow that would help me in case I ever had the crazy idea that I wanted to go back into this pit of hell, that if I only called upon God's help, he would be there to help me climb back out.

After getting out of treatment, I continued to attend meetings on a regular basis with others trying to remain sober, and I started volunteering on the unit where I had gone through treatment. It took some time to let the new-found freedom take root and start the new life with the right beginning. At that time, with Sue working and the Social Security Disability having been approved, we were not in dire financial straits, and that was the beginning of the first real stability with sobriety and employment.

A close friend of mine, now deceased, asked me to come to work for him selling sewing machines. I agreed to give it a try, and that was the beginning of a five-year association with him. He taught me the sewing machine business. I worked with him for about the first year and a half selling sewing machines. I also had enough freedom that it did not interfere with my weekly meetings and my volunteer work. Later, he and I branched out into the furniture business as well. We would find a store that wasn't doing so well, buy it and run a "going out of business" sale. We became partners in the furniture end of the business and did quite well.

Those years between 1974 and 1978 were great years for us. For the first time, I had steady employment and finances were no problem. As a family, we were in recovery together and it was a much happier time for all of us. Our youngest, Cindy, was still experiencing some problems in school but covering it up very well and denying any chemical use. We had concerns but couldn't pinpoint what was happening to her.

We had taken trips about every other year before, but most of them had been back to Richmond, Virginia, to visit Sue's family. We always had fun when we were with them, but we wanted to see more of the country as well. We began taking yearly vacations. These would include our oldest daughter's boyfriend, Steve, who would later become her husband. One vacation in particular was a houseboat trip to the Boundary Waters. We persuaded Sue's mom, aunt, and cousin to come with us. We rented a houseboat and took the girls and their friends. In all there were ten of us. It was the most relaxing, fun, exciting, exploring trip we had ever been on. We saw wildlife, including bears. We landed at a nudist colony when we were looking for directions. We cruised all over Kabatogama and Namakan lakes. We went out to dinner across the lake at a historic hotel that dated back to the early 1900s with the interior preserved in its original state. The furnishings dated back to the 1940s. We picked wild blueberries, and Sue's mom made a blueberry cobbler using a Pringles Potato Chip container to roll out the dough. We were frightened by a mama bear and her cub. We witnessed beautiful sunrises and sunsets. We docked on islands and ate hot dogs. We heard from someone on another houseboat that Richard Nixon had resigned as president of the United States. At the end of the week we were sad to have to leave such a beautiful, relaxing environment, but it was a wonderful experience, one about which we still reminisce almost forty years later. A few years later, we would take another houseboat trip into Canada with Sue's extended family and their children.

The next year Sue's family rented a large house at Nags Head, North Carolina, that would accommodate her immediate extended family. We invited a nun from Saint Benedict's

Fishing with my brother-in-law and Sue's mom in 1984. I'm running the motor.

Monastery who was a good friend. We rented a motor home, visited some of her family in Georgia and went on to Florida. There we went to Disneyland, Sea World, and Kennedy Space Center. After the week in Florida, we went up the coast to North Carolina and stayed in the motor home for a week, meeting Sue's family at Nags Head. Sharon had just graduated from high school and decided not to go on that trip with us as she was taking a trip to Florida with Steve and his brother and sister-in-law.

TWENTY

A New Demon Appears

Sometime in 1978, it seemed as though other demons had slowly crept into my life besides alcohol. I found I was working like I drank—to excess. I was becoming a workaholic instead of an alcoholic, working six full days and a half day on Sunday every week. We no longer had financial difficulties to cause a strain on family relationships, but my working all the time started to cause a problem because we never had any family time together. When I was at home, I was so tired, all I would do was eat and sleep. Once again, Sue and I seemed to be drifting apart. She was going one way and I another.

Karen had graduated from high school and was in her first year of college, and Cindy was in high school. My partner and I had bought and sold out several furniture stores. A short time after returning from one of our vacations, I came to find out there was a store for sale in Detroit Lakes, Minnesota. I took a drive up there and met with the owner. He wanted to sell the store and the building as well. My partner and I agreed to take over his furniture store. We paid him what he had paid for the furniture and agreed to advertise the sale of his building for him in the newspaper ads that we would run on a weekly basis for the furniture. I worked there six days a week for about three months. During that time, we did get a buyer for the building, a fact about which the owner was elated. We continued the going-out-of-business sale, and when I closed the place up, there was only one sofa left and a couple of miscellaneous items.

Upon my return home, I realized that if I didn't find something else to do, my marriage would be in real jeopardy. The time commitment it took to work the going-out-of-business sales was too great. In addition to that, I lacked time for participation in a recovery program. I was not able to spend time with my friends who were also in the recovery program. My volunteer work at the hospital was non-existent because I just didn't have the time. One Sunday, Sue came into the store and said, "I just can't take it like this any longer. You have to do something."
I found myself in a position of having to choose between my wife, my family and my current employment. I met with my partner and let him know I was leaving. It was that or lose Sue. So I quit the job and thought I would take some time to find out what other options I might have.

I had saved some money from all the furniture sales, so we were not financially strapped at the time. It really felt good to resume some quality time with the family and have some time to spend with my friends. I was able to resume my volunteer work on the addiction unit at the hospital. After about six months, the program director was in the process of collecting research data regarding alcohol treatment effectiveness. He approached me and asked if I wanted to help out with aftercare and the research in which he was involved. It was a volunteer position with reimbursement for the gas. My assignment was to visit ex-patients in their homes and interview them about how their recovery was going. I would report the information back to the director.

John, as a volunteer on the alcohol and drug unit at the St. Cloud Hospital.

During this time I had had another hip surgery and was back on Social Security Disability. Eventually I did some sales work and was able to get back off of disability. I had been volunteering at the hospital for about five years, and I was encouraged by the program director to seek a counselor training program. He felt I would make a good counselor. I certainly enjoyed working with alcoholics. I was talking to clients in the program, helping them to work on their recovery.

Since my accident and subsequent surgeries and having to be off and on disability, I was eligible for retraining in a different occupation. The program director suggested Hazelden Treatment Program in Center City, Minnesota, as a good place to gain the necessary counseling skills. He told me, upon my completion of the program, I would be licensed as an alcohol and chemical dependency counselor in the state of Minnesota. I decided to find out what

152

it would take to enroll. I drove to Hazelden to speak with the people in the training program. I found out that the program would take a year of training, and I would have to live on campus. I would get home every other weekend. That was pretty scary as it would mean I would have to leave Sue alone at home with the kids. She would need to continue to work, and I would be home only every other weekend. Sue had just decided she was going to begin taking a few college classes to further her education. After talking it over, we decided that I would go ahead and apply for the program, and Sue would forgo taking classes until I had finished the training program.

I filled out the application, sent it to Hazelden, and about three or four weeks later I was notified that I had been accepted into the counselor training program. Before entering, some personal interviews had been scheduled. Pending the outcome of those interviews, a final determination of acceptance would be made. I was interviewed by two counselors and a financial counselor who would determine if I had the financial ability to carry us through the one-year commitment it would take to complete the program. About one week after my return home, I was notified that I met all of the requirements and was accepted to start on March 10, 1979. I had about five months before my starting date to prepare for the training program.

I decided to do some more furniture sales, hoping to earn some additional money since I would not be working for over a year. I ran two sales during that five-month period, and they turned out quite well. That enabled me to enter the counselor training program quite confident that we would have enough money to get us by during those twelve-plus months. Sue stayed at home with Cindy and continued to work at the hospital. There was no way I could have made it through the program without her continued support. It was her sacrifice and employment that made it possible for me to go to school.

I grew anxious the closer the time came to enter the program. It was becoming more apparent that Cindy was having difficulties with school. At the time, she was attending St. John's Preparatory School in Collegeville, Minnesota. We were getting complaints about her behavior and her school work and were called in for a conference. It seemed that the consensus was that she was not applying herself and was hanging out with a guy who had been kicked out of school. He was suspected of bringing drugs on campus. Of course, Cindy denied it.

About a week later, she said she had to go to Saint John's for some required activity. For some reason, we didn't believe her but let her go anyway. A little later we drove out to Saint John's, and looking through the window outside of the cafeteria we saw her with the guy who had been kicked out of the school. We confronted them both, and they both denied being involved with any drugs or having anything to do with them. We also confronted her about lying to us about having an activity at school. She said that we were prejudging both of them, that he really was a nice guy, and she hated to be put in the position of having to lie to us. Sue and I went home, and Cindy came home about an hour later. I told her that if I ever found her with marijuana or any contraband in her possession, I would take her, along with the drugs, to the police department. It's not that our other children did not experience any difficulties, because they did. It just happened that Cindy was unfortunate enough to inherit the disease of chemical dependency.

It was not long until all of us were trying to get into the Christmas spirit. One of our traditions beginning when the girls were very small was that we would take them shopping for friends and ourselves on a Saturday sometime during the holidays. We would make a complete day of it and have lunch or dinner out with them. It always proved to be a fun-filled day. That year we had a great Christmas, and I started to prepare everyone for my departure to Hazelden.

TWENTY-ONE

The Training Program at Hazelden

I began the training program on March 10, 1979. It was tough. We had a lot of patient contact, a lot of studying and a lot of class work. The trainees had their own weekly group therapy sessions as well as various assignments from the trainers of the program. In addition, we had patients assigned to us and were responsible to do the initial intake work when a new patient arrived. We would present the intake work and our assessment to the counselor in charge, set appointments with the psychologist and take part in group therapy. We would have to do the documentation as well. On weekends, we would be in charge of the facility, with a counselor on call. If a problem arose, we could call and get direction as to how to handle the situation. If needed, the counselor would come in and assist us. Every other Friday, we could go home for a weekend. We reported back on Monday morning.

I'm sure that year dragged for Sue, yet for me time went by quickly. In no time at all, I was ready to start my last quarter at Hazelden, and I was assigned to the family program. I worked with spouses and family members of people who were in treatment. The family program was a week long and consisted of meetings, group therapy, and an interview with a psychologist to assess the patient's needs.

On one of my weekends home, there was a crisis with Cindy when we found marijuana in her purse. As a result, we carried out our threat of turning her in to the police for having a controlled substance. As she was almost eighteen years old at the time, it felt like the last opportunity we would have to get her some help. One of the most difficult and painful tough-love decisions we ever had to make was to follow through and take her down to the police station and turn her in.

The police released Cindy to our care. After taking her home, we gave her the choice of going to treatment at Hazelden or facing a judge. She chose treatment. I called Hazelden, made the arrangements and transported her with me on Monday morning. Cindy and I had an opportunity to talk on the way. She came to understand and admit that she needed help. I tried to give her all of the encouragement that I could. I let her know how much I loved her and was proud of her decision to enter treatment. Upon our arrival, I took her to the admissions office and we said our goodbyes.

She completed treatment successfully. I continued with my last quarter and was getting prepared for my graduation.

During my last quarter of treatment, Sue entered the family program at Hazelden for a week. By this time she had been in workshops and seminars on co-dependency. She, along with a nurse in the chemical dependency program, had developed a family program in St. Cloud. The Hazelden program proved to be extremely beneficial for Sue. She gained some new insights into herself and again experienced a deepening of her spiritual life.

I began putting out feelers for a job in the chemical dependency field and sending in applications. Once our exams were over and we received our certificates, I wanted to have a job to go to. I knew I could work in St. Cloud, but we were so far from Sue's family that I decided to see if I could find something closer to her home state of Virginia.

The time came for graduation. It was a very exciting get-together for all of the trainees and their families. We were all handed our certificates of completion. It was an emotional milestone for me. I couldn't believe it—only two and a half years of formal education, and I was able to complete a counselor training program with a college level curriculum!

I received a request for a job interview for a program director position in Baton Rouge, Louisiana, and went there for a interview. After the interview, I was given overnight to make a decision as to whether I would accept the job. Baton Rouge was still quite a distance from Virginia. I thought it over carefully that evening and realized I didn't feel ready to take over a treatment facility as program director when I was just fresh out of training. Fortunately, prior to my graduation, while still in training, I had given a presentation at the St. Cloud Hospital on chemical dependency and how the family could help break down the denial system in a patient. The presentation was well received. A while later, I received a letter of appreciation from the program director. When I returned to St. Cloud, I submitted an application for a counselor position on the unit. I was hired and began my new career as a chemical dependency counselor.

TWENTY-TWO

My Position at St. Cloud Hospital

When I returned to St. Cloud, I submitted an application for employment on the A & C Unit. After about two weeks, the program director asked me to come in and interview for a counselor position. He asked if I would be willing to be a replacement counselor for the summer and fill in wherever needed when people went on vacation. I agreed to take the position and started work shortly thereafter.

Having volunteered at the A&C unit for years, I was pretty familiar with the surroundings. I was assigned an office and started work right away. The counseling staff had been waiting to take their vacations and were happy I came on board. This made it possible for them to take time off.

I had been working as the fill-in counselor for about three or four months when I was asked if I would take over the Aftercare coordinator position. The person who had the position was being moved to another department, leaving a vacancy in Aftercare. After giving it some thought, I agreed to take it on.

Aftercare consisted of patients who had been through treatment and would return to the hospital on a weekly basis, along with their spouses to participate in a group made up of about twelve people. Here they were able to come together each week for support and to share their progress or difficulties encountered during the week. Patients would talk about how their sobriety was going, and spouses were able to share what it was like for them now that the alcoholic was no longer drinking. They would also share how they were dealing with the new lifestyle of sobriety. The non-alcoholic most often had taken over many of the responsibilities of the family and the discipline of the children. Now, with a sober spouse, many found it hard to give up much of the control, especially when it came to finances. They found it hard to trust that the alcoholic wouldn't drink again.

Many times the children had learned to react to the drinking in negative ways, often siding with one or the other parent. Aftercare gave both parties a place to talk about their strengths, weaknesses, successes, failures, hopes, and dreams they were experiencing on a weekly basis. Sharing their happier times was always welcome. When problems would arise, or when another group member had experienced a similar situation, that person would share how they had dealt with it, thus giving encouragement and support to one another.

When I took over as Aftercare coordinator, we had about thirty to thirty-five people participating in the program. When I left three and a half years later, I had 175 people coming to Aftercare on a weekly basis. I trained twenty-eight facilitators who had been through the treatment program. They, in turn, would facilitate a group of about twelve people. I would have anywhere from twelve to fifteen groups meeting each week on Wednesday evening.

I loved what I was doing, yet it was beginning to take a toll on me. It seemed every week there was a client contemplating suicide. I would have to meet with the individual and determine whether he or she needed to be hospitalized or referred to the

Mental Health Center. It was possible that all they needed was to be referred to a counselor of their choice to help them deal with their emotional instability and give them additional help with their problem.

I also started the St. Cloud Hospital Alcohol and Chemical Addiction Unit Alumni Association. It started with a core group from the Aftercare program interested in finding activities for people who wanted to stay sober and have fun at the same time. The group had good ideas but no funds to implement them, but they were fearless and determined. We decided to go out on a limb and have a celebration of sobriety.

We wanted to bring in a well-known speaker in the field of alcohol and chemical dependency (in the early days alcohol and other chemicals were separated). We advertised the event as A Celebration of Sobriety, hoping to draw participants from surrounding areas, as well as St. Cloud. Father Joseph Martin was considered an expert in the field of alcoholism. He was a much sought after speaker. He had written a booklet on each of the Twelve Steps of Alcoholism being used in treatment centers, as well as many other documents on the subject. I contacted Fr. Martin, and he agreed to come and speak. We booked him and rented Hallenbeck Hall at St. Cloud State University to hold the event. We advertised around town and sent flyers to AA Clubs in surrounding areas, hoping to sell enough tickets to cover the expenses of the event. The group was very excited and worked very hard. When we sold over 1,000 tickets, everyone was jumping for joy.

Two days before the event, I got a call from Fr. Martin's secretary stating that he was very ill and unable to attend. Here we were expecting over 1,000 people and our speaker wasn't going to be there. It was too late to cancel the event. I remembered a priest we had heard speak in Winnipeg, Canada, who might be a good substitute. I contacted him and asked if he would be willing to fly in and be the featured speaker on such short notice. He agreed to come.

The night of the event the program director went up to the podium and announced to the crowd how sorry we were that Fr. Martin would be unavailable, due to illness, and hoped that they would understand. If anyone wanted their money returned, we would be glad to do so. Even though the people were somewhat disappointed, they were quite gracious and accepted the explanation. Only one person came up and asked for a refund which was given. What a relief that was.

After the event was over and all the expenses were paid, we made about $5,000 in profit. That was the seed money that enabled us to form a committee to help find and appoint people to run for the board of the A&C Alumni Association. After the Alumni Association Board was formed, I took the treasurer to the bank and opened an account with the profits from the Celebration of Sobriety event. As I had a full plate with my position as Aftercare Coordinator, I didn't want the responsibility of the Alumni Association and turned it over to the board. I agreed to stay in the background and be available when needed.

The Association did quite well and started holding regular sober events. They would rent the senior citizens center on a Friday night for dances, go bowling as a group, have parties on holidays and sometimes go to a play. They would sponsor weekend campouts where they would rent a Greyhound bus and go away for the weekend. The whole group would cook out and have a good time socializing. We would have camp fires in the evening, roast marshmallows and hot dogs, while someone played a guitar or we would just enjoy the peace and tranquility of setting around a campfire.

One Saturday night it stormed. When people came out of their tents in the morning, they were laughing and singing as they wrung water out of their sleeping bags. We took big yard garbage bags and made rain gear out of them to stay dry. Everyone would return home on Sunday afternoon feeling rejuvenated and ready to start a fresh week.

Fees for these activities were minimal. We found these were great ways to help alcoholics in their early sobriety realize they could have fun without drinking.

It was sometime in about 1980 that Blue Cross and Blue Shield Insurance Company started a program called Effective Care 81 and began scrutinizing all treatment centers. They reviewed the documentation that had been submitted for payment to determine what criteria had been documented to justify keeping a patient in treatment for an average of ninety days. Blue Cross then established criteria on which chemical dependency reimbursement would be based.

The insurance companies were beginning to put more and more pressure on the providers to do more with less. They were no longer willing to continue to provide treatment for ninety-day inpatient stays without documenting the medical necessity for a stay of that duration. Most treatment was being cut back to thirty to forty-five days. In extreme cases of debilitation, it might have taken thirty days for a person to stabilize enough to participate in treatment.

Outpatient treatment was just coming into being. People would come in five nights a week for three hours and participate in treatment on an out-patient basis while living at home. This was a new concept in chemical dependency treatment, and the third party payers were leaning towards this as a first line of defense. If the client failed to stay chemically free during or after an out-patient program, a referral would be made to enter a more in-depth, inpatient treatment program.

Aftercare was growing, yet, I was the only staff person. One evening I had seven people who were potentially suicidal. Since I was the only staff available, I had each person call his or her pastor and ask if they could be seen right away. I was getting burned out and decided I had to do something to take care of myself. One of the things we learned to ask ourselves in counselor training was, "Who takes care of the caregiver?" The answer to that was that we had to learn to take care of ourselves.

My wife and daughters had become involved with a program called TEC (Teens Encounter Christ, now called Together Encountering Christ) and were encouraging me to go on a TEC retreat weekend. I was dragging my feet. They took the ball in their court and paid for a TEC weekend as a birthday present for me. When the time came, I went and was quite impressed with the program. The weekend was made up of about seventy percent teens, sixteen years and above, and about thirty percent adults. I know my participation in the program helped me spiritually. It seemed to be a wonderful, enriching weekend for ninety-nine and nine-tenths of the participants. I was enthused about the weekend.

After a period of time working with various aspects of the program, Sue and I were encouraged to become lay directors for a weekend. After that, we worked many more weekends for a period of about seven or eight years. As a result of that program, I not only grew spiritually, but I learned more ways to deal with the stress at work and learned to trust that, if I would but turn my life over, God would lead me on a different path.

TWENTY-THREE

The Move to Duluth

The situation at work was not improving and was becoming more taxing as time went on. The problems I was facing with clients continued to mount, and I was becoming more burned out. Sue and I talked, and, with her support, I made a decision to look for another job. A friend of mine whom I had worked for previously asked if I would come back and sell sewing machines. I took the position and was there about a year and a half working in and around St. Cloud.

During that time, I discovered that Duluth, Minnesota, did not have representation for the brand of sewing machines we were selling. After some investigation, Sue and I decided to open our own sewing machine store in Duluth. At first we would work it on a trial basis. Sue would stay in St. Joseph until we could see if the store would support us. Since it was a retail store, we kept it open on Saturdays. Sue would either come up there for the weekend or I would go home to St. Joseph after closing on Saturday and go back early Monday morning.

After about six months, the store was doing very well, and we decided to sell the house in St. Joseph. Sue kept her job and stayed part time at the hospital for another six months before resigning.

After the house was sold, we bought a new home on a lake in Fredenburg Township about twenty miles outside of Duluth. We totally remodeled it. After remodeling the house, it was beautiful, and we loved it. It was situated on a hill overlooking the lake, and the front of the house had lots of windows. We could enjoy the scenery from anywhere in the house, had a garden in the back and occasionally we could see deer from our window. It truly was a serene setting. Sue loved the quiet and enjoyed staying at home. After working on the A&C Unit for fifteen years, she too found that

she had become burned out and needed a change. God works in mysterious ways. Often, when we can't seem to break away, even when we need to, we are forced into a situation of change. Eventually, Sue got a very good part-time job as the Fredenburg Town Clerk.

Our days in Duluth were filled with joy for the most part. By this time we had seven grandchildren, and they would visit us at various times. In the summer we would pick berries with them. The little boys would make forts and cut down branches to make a path

John and Sue in Duluth, 1990.

165

to the neighbors, while the girls would help Sue in the kitchen cooking and baking. They learned to fish, and Grandpa was always ready to take them out. In the wintertime we would make snowmen and go sledding. Sometimes Grandma would be on the bottom of the sled with several of the children piled on the top of her. The grandchildren were so close in age they were a delight. We always anticipated their coming for about two weeks beforehand. When they said goodbye, we would put our feet up and relax. It was always wonderful to have them come, but we would find it very tiring trying to keep up with them and keep them entertained. We enjoyed family gatherings, especially around holidays and always tried to make them special.

After a while, for no apparent reason, business started falling off. I had to increase the advertising to bring in more customers. Advertising costs were high and, while with more advertising we would get a little more business, we would not get enough to cover the overhead and also take money out for living expenses. After about two years we decided it didn't make sense to continue, as we were going further in debt financially. We held a going-out-of-business sale and closed the doors of the Duluth Sewing Center.

TWENTY-FOUR

Medjugorje

About that time, some friends told us about a village in Yugoslavia called Medjugorje, where the Blessed Virgin Mary was supposedly visiting five children on a daily basis, giving them messages about the need for change if we were to find peace. The apparitions had been going on for some time when we heard about them, and people were already going there on pilgrimages. They would spend a week in the village, living among the population and visionaries. People would go over to pray and reconcile themselves with God, and, yes, to visit with some of the visionaries as well. Three of our good friends were planning to go and encouraged us to go with them. Sue and I had enough money for one of us to go to Yugoslavia, but not enough for both of us. I tried to encourage Sue. She felt that I needed to go more than she did, and we began to make plans for me to go.

One of our friends was taking his son; his wife was staying back also. She called Sue and said, "But what if we're supposed to go?" While praying the rosary about the trip, Sue's chain on her rosary turned from silver to gold. This was the sign she needed to know that she was supposed to go with me on the pilgrimage. Now we just had to figure out how to finance the trip for her.

About five years before that we had bought a nice boat that we used for fishing. I got in touch with my daughter, Karen, in St. Cloud because I knew she wanted my boat. I asked her if she and her husband wanted to buy the boat. They said, "Yes," and that gave us the money so that Sue and I could go on the pilgrimage together. As long as we were going to Yugoslavia, I

John enjoying fishing.

thought that it would be a perfect time for me to try to go back to Poland and see if I could find the house I had lived in as a child.

I thought I could find it. I could extend the trip to Yugoslavia by a week and go on to Poland. I would have to drive through Czechoslovakia, which was under communist control and did not want to expose Sue to unnecessary danger. I would have to drive from Zagreb, Yugoslavia, through Austria, and Czechoslovakia and into Poland. We decided that's what I would do, and Sue would go back to the States with the tour group.

The trip to Medjugorje was another spiritually deep, life-changing experience for both Sue and me. We witnessed miracles before our eyes, talked to the villagers and found a reverence among the people that does not exist here in the States. The church was always packed with people standing outside listening to the Mass being said over loudspeakers. There were several Masses daily in different languages, and they were always

packed. We climbed the mountains praying along the way with the rest of the pilgrims. Before we knew it, the week was over and it was time for Sue to go home and for me to continue on to Poland.

John and Sue board the bus to begin our trip to Medjugorje.

TWENTY-FIVE

Foiled Trip to Poland

I had rented a car through Hertz that would be available to me at the airport in Yugoslavia on the completion of our pilgrimage. We went to Zagreb together and said our goodbyes at the airport. Sue gave me what we thought was my airline ticket before she got on the plane for her direct flight to Chicago. As I got to the Hertz Rental Agency, I looked at my ticket and discovered I had Sue's airline ticket, and she had mine. Here I was in Yugoslavia with her ticket, wondering if I would be able to get back home with it. I walked over to the airline desk and told the agent what happened. The agent said not to worry that I would be fine and would be able to fly with that ticket back to the United States. I went back to Hertz, picked up the car and started on my drive to Poland.

I drove across Austria. It was a beautiful, beautiful country. It was bringing back memories and deep feelings for a part of the planet that I had yearned to see again. When I got to the Czechoslovakian border, there were guards with machine guns, which brought back memories long buried, along with old fears. I stopped at the checkpoint. The guard took my papers and motioned for me to get out of the car. There were a lot of hand motions as we tried to make each other understood. He motioned for me to open the trunk, which I did, and wanted me to open the suitcase.

Before leaving the United States, I had bought extra cigarettes and big packages of chewing gum that held about twenty individual packs and put them in a cellophane bag. I remembered how I was able to bribe guards as a child. I went on instinct and gave one of those chewing gum bags to the guard. He returned my papers, shut the suitcase and trunk and waved me through.

I kept driving for about three hours. Every village had red flags with the hammer and cycle, and some of the buildings were painted with the markings as well. There was not a doubt about who was in control. I came to a fork in the road and was going to turn right. But, as I reached the fork, police officers with machine guns motioned for me to pull over. They looked at my international driver's license and my passport. We tried to understand each other with a lot of hand waves. They kept saying, "radar, radar," and "speeding."

I just smiled for there was no radar. They issued me a ticket and wanted sixty dollars. I didn't have any Czechoslovakian money, so they motioned to a village which I could see about a mile up the road. The policeman repeatedly said, "hotel," and pointed toward the village.

They held my passport while I drove to the hotel and exchanged my traveler's check into Czechoslovakian money and then drove back out to the checkpoint. When I paid the fine, they returned my passport. By that time it was about 8:00 p.m. I was tired and hungry, so I decided to stay in the hotel for the night. I went in and got a sandwich and went to the desk to check into a room.

The person at the desk could speak broken English, and I asked for an explanation about the radar and what was going on out there. She laughed and said, "Today, Friday. Everybody pay."

I guess the locals were quite used to it, as that's the way the police made their salary for the week. The only difference was that I had an American passport, and it cost me sixty dollars, and for the locals they charged ten dollars.

The next morning I got up, had something to eat, and, as I pondered the fine, I had to chuckle over the experience with the police as I drove on to Poland. There was no problem crossing the border into Poland. I know I had tears in my eyes. I was back in the country of my birth. I drove on and gave a little boy a ride to his home, which was about two miles from where I picked him up. I know it made his day.

I continued on to my hometown—Lodz, Poland. I checked into a hotel and went to my room to freshen up a little from the drive before going to the restaurant for dinner. I had planned to ask someone at the front desk if they knew of anyone I could hire who could speak fluent Polish and English, but I was tired and decided to wait until morning. I went back to my room and started looking over my passport. I happened to look at the Czechoslovakian visa and discovered I had a single entry visa for Czechoslovakia. That meant that I had used up my visa when I traveled across Czechoslovakia, and I had no way to get back. It was not a round trip visa. I thought, *Wow, this is great. I'm in Poland, but I've got no way to get back across to Czechoslovakia.* I had rented the car in Yugoslavia and had to drive it back and turn it in before my return flight to the United States, which meant I'd have to drive back across Czechoslovakia.

The next morning I got on the telephone with the American Embassy in Warsaw and explained my situation. I was told that I had better come to Warsaw right away and get it straightened out as it could take some time. I was disappointed that I had to leave Lodz without an opportunity to do some investigating into my background or the opportunity to find the home I lived in as a child. This was the second time in my life I had gone back to Lodz in hopes of finding the home I knew as a child and was unable to do so.

I checked out of the hotel, got in the car and drove to Warsaw. Upon my arrival, I checked into the Intercontinental Hotel, which was my first priority. I then decided I would take a taxi because I didn't know how to get around Warsaw. We got to the embassy, and I told the driver to wait for me as I went inside. I talked to an official. He explained that the relationship with the Czechoslovakian embassy was very poor, and I had better go over there and make arrangements to get a visa to get back across.

I left the American embassy, got back into the cab and had the driver take me to the Czechoslovakian embassy. The official there gave me some papers to fill out, and when I went to hand them back to him, he said it was going to cost ten American dollars for a visa, and I needed a passport picture. I got back in the cab and had the driver take me to the hotel where I explained my problem. Since none of the banks or hotels in Poland would give out American money, the manager, who was very kind, cashed a traveler's check for me.

The manager said he would introduce me to a man who would know where to take me to get a passport picture. This man explained it would take three days to obtain the picture once the photographer had taken it. He agreed to take me to the photographer. I was quite anxious to get the picture because I knew I had to drive back to Yugoslavia and get on the plane for the United States on Friday. I was surprised to find that things are quite different in Europe. Here we are used to instant pictures—walking into a booth, putting a quarter in and getting a passport picture.

On the third day after getting my picture taken, the driver came back to pick me up to go get the pictures and then take me over to the Czechoslovakian embassy. Once there, I gave the embassy the pictures with the papers and ten dollars of American money. The official stamped and signed the visa and handed it to me. I think I gave a sigh of relief at that point. I thanked him and walked back out. I got into the car, and we went back to the hotel where I paid the driver and went up to my room.

I needed some time by myself to try to sort things out and decide how I was going to get back to Zagreb. I decided to spend the night, get up in the morning and start driving back. I would try to go as far in one day as I could. I didn't want to get hung up again and take the chance of being delayed. I had to allow myself some extra time in case something extreme or unforeseen happened getting across Czechoslovakia and the border. The next morning after breakfast I loaded the car and started heading toward Czechoslovakia.

When I got to the border, it was not a problem getting into Czechoslovakia from Poland. Poland was still under communist control, as well as Czechoslovakia, and had better relations. Therefore, they were more accommodating at their borders. I continued on and made my way across the border into Austria where, at the check-point crossing, there wasn't even a guard present. I drove across into Austria without being stopped. I gave a big sigh of relief and drove on to Yugoslavia.

My guardian angel was really watching out for me that day. I made it out of the communist controlled countries and on into a democratic nation again. I kept driving and arrived in Zagreb about nine o'clock that evening. I saw a sign that said Holiday Inn, and decided to rent a room there for the night. After eating dinner, I went up to my room to bed. I had experienced a full day, one that would stay with me for a long time to come. I allowed myself an extra day in case I ran into trouble. It was nice to have the extra time to rest up for the flight home. I knew that when I got on the airplane it was a nonstop flight to Chicago.

The following day I returned the rental car to Hertz and went over to the airline counter. I presented my ticket and everything went smoothly. No one said a word. I must have looked like a Sue, since I had her ticket. The agent told me which gate I needed and when to be there. I didn't have long to wait. In just a couple hours, they started to board the aircraft. I got into my seat, and soon we were off to the United States. What a relief to be going home! After my arrival in Chicago, I again went to the United Airlines Ticket Counter and showed them my ticket, told them what had happened and was assured that everything would be fine. They told me at what gate I would be boarding, and I went there. A short time later, I boarded the plane for home.

Sue and Sharon were at the airport in Minneapolis waiting for me. I told them I was never so glad to set foot on American soil as I was that evening. At Sharon's house that night, I shared the experience of the problems I had encountered in Czechoslovakia with the visa, the fiasco in Poland that prevented me from having time to check on my ancestry, how I was finally able to get the visa straightened out and, on top of all of that, I was flying home on Sue's plane ticket. We could laugh about it then, even though it was extremely frightening at the time it was taking place. After spending the night we headed for our home in Duluth.

TWENTY-SIX

Back to the Job Market

Back in Duluth I knew I was going to have to do something to make a living. I started to job search again and found what I thought was an interesting sales position advertised in the *USA Today Newspaper*. It was selling energy-saving devices for a company out of California. I checked into the company and decided that I would give that a try. I got the information from the company in California and, after talking to them at length and looking over some of the devices they were selling, I decided to give it a try.

In the meantime, the owner of Maji Travel, the agency that had booked our Medjugorje pilgrimage to Yugoslavia, called and asked if we would be willing to take telephone calls and speak about our personal experience at a presentation for upcoming trips. Later, I was asked if I would be a tour escort. I had the opportunity to make two more of these trips.

Our guides in Medjugorje were excellent. They directed all the activities while we were there. The group would gather under a designated tree outside of church, and I would give them schedules of events for the day with instructions. Then I would turn the group over to the Yugoslavia tour guide. Some of the planned activities were to take the group to visit the visionaries at their home, take a walk up Apparition Hill and climb Cross Mountain.

Apparition Hill was the place the Blessed Virgin Mary first appeared to the children. On our journey up Cross Mountain, we learned about the history of the cross on top of the mountain. The visionaries would go to Cross Mountain and stop and pray at the various Stations of the Cross as they climbed up the mountain. One evening, after I had just completed dinner, I ventured out on the balcony. I looked toward Cross Mountain and saw the cross illuminated in red. As I gazed upon the cross, it struck me that there was no electricity on that mountain, and the cross could not have been illuminated by natural means. I went back inside and called our group, which was having dinner, and told them to come and look at the cross. They all witnessed the same illumination as I did.

Mountain of the Cross, Mt. Krizevac, Medjugorje, Yugoslavia, 1988.

One of the women in our group was determined to go to Cross Mountain to pray. I thought it was too dangerous of a journey for her to make alone. The climb up the mountain was rugged and dangerous, so I told her I would go with her. We got flashlights and started out. By the time we got to the base of the mountain, she had no battery left in her flashlight. As we started up the mountain, we stopped at each station to pray and to rest. It was very dark, and we could not see to the right or left of the path; only the path itself was illuminated by the moon. When we stepped off the path, we would say a prayer, and I needed to turn my flashlight on to see where we were going. When we stepped back onto the path, it was as if the path was being illuminated for us.

On the way up the mountain, the cross was not visible to us. When we got to the top, there was only one candle sitting at its base burning, and the cross was not illuminated as we had witnessed from the balcony when we were having dinner. We spent a few minutes in prayer at the foot of the cross and started our journey down the mountain. About half way down, I started to fall, face forward, but before I hit the ground, it was as if some force held me up to lessen the impact. I did not even receive a scratch. We continued to the bottom of the mountain, and, as we turned around and looked up, once again the cross was illuminated in red.

We did meet the visionaries. One evening I was privileged to be part of a small group of people allowed up in the balcony during an apparition of one of the visionaries. The visionary who had the apparition was a young boy about fifteen years old. He faced the wall at the appointed time, knelt down and started praying the "Hail Mary." After about the first sentence, his lips kept moving as if he were carrying on a conversation with no actual words coming out of his mouth. He seemed oblivious to what was going on around him. The balcony of Saint James

Church was very still and quiet. At times he would say nothing and seemed to be listening. And then his lips would move as if he were responding, but again, he made no sound. This continued on for approximately seventeen minutes. Then we could hear his words again speaking the "Hail Mary" where he had left off before the apparition started. I believe the boy was in communication with the Blessed Virgin Mary.

Before one of my later trips to Medjugorje, I had purchased a battery-operated car to give to one of the children and, as I was going through customs at the Zagreb, Yugoslavia, airport, I was stopped and motioned to a different area, where the security guards searched me and my suitcase. After finding the battery-operated car, they were satisfied that I was not a threat entering their country. I barely caught up with the rest of the group for whom I was responsible on the tour. After arrival in Dubrovnik, Yugoslavia, we were again reminded that we were in a communist country when one of the people with our group was seen taking pictures. A guard came over, took her camera and smashed it. I ushered the group into the terminal, as they were becoming frightened, and excited. I instructed them not to say anything to the guards. It was a good reminder for all of us of the freedoms we were allowed in our country that were ignored and trampled on in countries that have no freedom.

As I reflect on the experiences I encountered during my journeys to Medjugorje, they deepened my faith and reinforced my belief in a life hereafter in a place with the God of my understanding.

TWENTY-SEVEN

More Surgery

In 1989, upon my return home from Medjugorje, I began selling and installing energy-saving devices for a company out of California. I made an appointment to do an energy audit and cost estimate for a grocery store chain. When I arrived, the store manager directed me to the location where the device was to be installed. I entered a dark room, feeling around for a light switch. I could not find the switch on the wall. However, I looked up and could make out a white string hanging from a light fixture in the ceiling. I took a step into the room to reach for the string and, as I did, I fell into a huge, uncovered hole that was probably three feet wide, four feet long and four feet deep. As I fell into the hole I extended my arms out and caught myself but, my right leg got twisted up behind me. It happened to be the same leg for which I had had all the previous hip surgeries. When I was hanging in the hole, supported by my arms, I was in excruciating pain, and I started to holler loudly for help. Someone heard me and came to pull me out of the hole. I had them help me out to the car and managed to drive home.

Upon my arrival at home, Sue and our daughter Karen, who was visiting from St. Cloud, brought my crutches and helped me out of the car. I could not stand on the leg at all, and they convinced me to go to the Emergency Room at the hospital in Duluth. When I got there, my leg was X-rayed; this showed that there was a hairline fracture of the femur. The orthopedic surgeon put my leg in a cast, ordered a hospital bed to be delivered to our home and explained that I would be bedridden for the next six weeks.

Once again, I was prescribed pain medication and needed to continue to take it to make the pain somewhat bearable. I had a hard time sleeping at night because of the pain. I would get up and sit at the kitchen counter in the middle of the night and play solitaire for hours to help keep my mind off of the pain I was experiencing. This went on for about three to six months and my leg was not getting better.

The orthopedic surgeon knew the head of the orthopedic department at the University of Minnesota and assured me that this surgeon was an expert and knew what he was doing. There was no choice but for me to have the surgery, and we needed to make difficult financial decisions. We talked it over with our girls. Sharon and Steve offered to have us move in with them in Prior Lake until we could get on our feet. We knew that the recovery period from this surgery was going to be a very lengthy one. We had no choice but to accept their generous offer and move to Prior Lake. We sold our house and most of our possessions. We then said "Good-bye" to the place we had grown to love and tearfully left for Prior Lake at the beginning of July 1990. Sue and I experienced a lot of personal growth as we shared the joys and tragedies that took place while living in Duluth.

Soon after we moved to Prior Lake, I faced another major hip revision operation. I had the surgery, but even before I left the hospital, I knew that something wasn't right with my hip. However, the doctor didn't seem to be concerned. Again, I found I needed to go back on Social Security Disability.

We were asked if we would be willing to help take care of Sharon and Steve's children and a friend's child after school for a couple of hours a day until the parents got home from work. We enjoyed the children, and life seemed to be settling down.

In November of that same year, Millie called to tell us that Willard Van Vickle had died after being sick for a very long time. Even though we knew his time on earth was limited, no one expected him to die as quickly as he did. I was completely devastated. The person who had rescued me, befriended me, loved me and given me a home was now gone. To this day I miss him very much. It was good that Sue and I had the responsibility of the children after school as it helped ease the pain from all the losses we were still experiencing.

We lived in Prior Lake for about three and a half years. During that time, I tried a few different sales jobs and discovered that having to walk distances was too difficult because I was still experiencing a lot of pain with my leg.

TWENTY-EIGHT

Truckin' Along Again

I figured I could go back to driving a truck again as long as I did not have to handle any freight or do any type of lifting. I was fortunate to land a job with Tri-Action Trucking Company. They were running all brand-new equipment, which made it very attractive because the equipment was designed for over-the-road driving. This meant that it had the best interior and the best seating equipment: air-ride cab, air-ride frame, and pulling air-ride trailers, making it possible for minimal fatigue for the driver. I started driving for them, and it went quite well.

I let it be known at the beginning that I had a problem with my leg and would not be able to lift, load or unload trucks. If it ever came to a load I could not manage, I would have to hire someone to help. They assured me that would be no problem, and it wasn't. They liked the job I was doing as I always managed to be on time, and they never had any complaints from customers about any of the loads I delivered.

Tri-Action encouraged their drivers to purchase trucks and lease them back to the company. After driving for about a year, I had been able to save enough money to make a down payment on a truck, which I leased back to them. For me, it was a dream fulfilled. Tri-Action bought the license, insurance, tires and paid the maintenance. In addition, they paid me $2,000 a month to lease the truck back to them. It proved to be a good investment. We were able to save enough money to eventually get back out on our own.

Shortly thereafter, Sue's sister Gail called to tell us that their mother was ill and having trouble with dementia and short-term memory loss. Gail had always planned to have Mom live with her once she could no longer live independently. Sue decided to go to Richmond to help with her care. It was soon evident that her mother was not going to be able to return home. She would not hear of staying at Gail's because all she wanted to do was to be back in her own home.

The family had a decision to make. After much thought and facing the reality of Mom's condition, the decision was made that, for her safety, she would need to move into an assisted living facility and did so within a few months. It was a very sad time for all of us.

Shortly after Mom was moved and settled, Sue called and said she was ready to come home and could I come and get her. I was able to get a trip to Richmond with a return trip back to Minneapolis. We loaded Sue's belongings in the truck and headed for home. I was fortunate to be driving a truck at that time, as I could request to be dispatched to and from Richmond whenever I needed to be.

Gail and her husband, Don, were very faithful. They visited every day and would take Mom to their home on weekends. If they couldn't be there, they would see to it that one of the brothers would visit her. We made the trip to Richmond two or three times a year until Mom's death in 2004 at the age of ninety-three. She was a grand lady, a very proud and ingenious woman who always enjoyed a good time. She worked very hard her whole life for her family. As I reflect back, we did have much in common. Her family was the most important thing in her life, just as my family is for me.

We returned to Prior Lake and soon realized we all needed our space. We had been working diligently to save enough money to get back on our own and made the decision to move back to St. Cloud.

Karen was managing an apartment complex in Waite Park and said they were in need of someone to clean the buildings and encouraged Sue to take the job. The apartments were nice. There was one on the ground floor near the entrance, and we decided to take it. Sue worked at the complex for about three months and then began looking for work in St. Cloud. It just so happened that there was an opening on Recovery Plus, formerly called the A&C Unit, where she had worked so many years prior to moving to Duluth. It was only part time, but they were happy to have her back. In no time at all, she was working full time. She continued working at Recovery Plus for another twelve years until her retirement in 2005.

TWENTY-NINE

Health Problems

I continued leasing and driving my truck for Tri-Action. Things seemed to be going quite well for us when we were faced with a new medical crisis. After we had been back in St. Cloud about three to four months, I was out on a run when I pulled something in my groin. I started feeling uncomfortable and thought I should have it checked out. I made an appointment, went to the doctor and was told I needed to have surgery for a hernia repair. I was told that I could have the surgery and be out within a day. He set up the necessary examination that needed to be done prior to surgery, which included a chest X-ray and then scheduled the surgery. The next day I received a phone call. It was the doctor asking me to come to his office. When I arrived, he informed me that the X-ray revealed a spot on my lung. He explained that it was small, about the size of a dime in circumference, but I needed to get that checked out. Instead of going to the hospital for hernia surgery, he scheduled me for exploratory lung surgery.

I remember the ride to the hospital on the morning of the surgery. I lit up a cigarette, which would be the last cigarette I would smoke. The doctor came in and talked to me in the hospital room and said he planned to do the exploratory surgery. He explained that if the spot should be cancerous, they would take out two-thirds of my lung. He said it would hardly affect me at all, and I could lead a normal life. It didn't sound like the procedure was going to be much of a problem, and I signed the papers agreeing to the surgery. The surgery took seven and a half hours. When I awoke, I was shocked to learn that they removed two-thirds of my right lung due to cancer and was told that the surgery had gone well. It was a couple of hours later when I thought I could hear air when I inhaled and exhaled. It seemed like something was leaking.

The next morning the doctor came in and listened to my chest. He told me I would have to be taken back into surgery because the lung had developed a leak. He called Sue at work and informed her of the problem. She called the girls, and again they waited while I was taken back into surgery. After about another seven hours of surgery, the doctor came out looking very downcast. He informed them that he could not get the leak stopped, and, therefore, he had been unable to save the remaining part of my lung. When I went in for the second surgery, I hadn't thought it was going to be much. I just thought they were going to sew the leak shut, and that would be it. When I woke up and tried to move, I could hardly breathe. I was told that the surgeon had to remove the rest of the lung because he could not get the leak stopped. I was terrified and had no clue how this news would affect my life or what it would mean for my future.

There were times during my stay in the hospital that I really became frightened when I tried to do something and realized I couldn't. The first time I tried to summon a nurse when I couldn't breathe, I found I didn't have the strength to roll over and press the call button. I was gasping for air when a nurse opened the door, and I was able to tell her that I needed oxygen. She turned the oxygen up to a higher flow so that I could breathe. After that, either Sue or one of the girls stayed with me around the clock until I was able to go home again.

The doctor came in the next morning and apologized. He said there really wasn't anything he could do to save the lung. He had done everything he could, but the leak would not stop. He also explained that the biggest concern during this recovery would be the development of pneumonia. He told me I would have to cooperate with the nurses and therapists, who would be in on a regular schedule to have me cough, so that my other lung would not fill with fluid. On the second day after surgery, they had me standing up at the side of the bed and taking a few steps in the room and then put me back into bed. On the third and fourth day I graduated to walking with an oxygen tank in the hall for a little bit at a time. When I got to the door, I thought I would try a little toe tapping, and soon found out I couldn't do much of anything. It was really slow and difficult because it took all I could do to breathe and to take a step.

By the end of the week, I was back at home with instructions for a recovery program that included walking on a daily basis. Since Karen was managing the apartment complex, she was able to ask the maintenance men to keep an eye on me when I went out for a walk. I kept increasing the walk day by day, and in a short time, I could walk about two blocks which was quite an achievement for me. I was determined I wasn't going to let this conquer me.

I could no longer continue to drive my truck. I soon found out that Tri-Action was on the verge of bankruptcy. Therefore, even if I hired a driver, unless I leased it to another company, the truck would no longer be able to produce an income for us. Due to my health issues, we made the decision to sell the truck. But buying it proved to have been a good investment as we were able to sell it for a profit.

Once again, I was faced with the need to go back on Social Security Disability. The recovery from the lung surgery was extremely long and painful due to the fact that they had to cut through ribs, muscles and tendons to get at the lung, and everything had to heal from the inside. It took about eighteen months before I began feeling fairly good again and the pain began to decrease.

I loved to fish, and a friend of ours had a trailer on a lake and would sometimes take me fishing with him during my recovery. There was a trailer for sale with a pontoon boat, and we decided it would be a good investment. We could drive up on weekends and enjoy getting out of town, fishing and having a place to relax.

We had some great times. Sometimes the kids would come up on weekends and bring their trailers, and we would love having the grandchildren around again, just as we had experienced in Duluth when they were much younger. They would build a fire in the evening and sit out by the campfire for hours telling stories, playing games and singing until the wee hours of the morning. I was always tired at the end of the day and unable to sit by the fire because of the smoke, so I would turn in after dinner. Sue always enjoyed having the company because when they weren't around we didn't make a fire. She and I would just play a game or two in the trailer before turning in for the evening.

The lake was a great place for the grandkids. By this time we had eight of them, and they ranged in age from about seven to thirteen. Every year I would take the boys for a week. It would be just the boys and myself. Our son-in-law John would bring a speed boat and leave it so I could pull the kids around on inner tubes and let them try to water ski. The two older ones were able to help with chores, especially those things that were too difficult for me and took too much energy. I would do the cooking, and they would do the dishes. I would take them fishing on the pontoon, take them out swimming, and they always had a great time. I would let them build a fire. As I watched from the screened porch they roasted hotdogs and marshmallows and made s'mores. They would sleep outside in tents.

The first year, the youngest, who had never been away from mom and dad overnight, got homesick, and I had to bring

Lake Vermillion, 1999. Left to right: Cindy, Daren, Sharon, Sue, and John.

him into the trailer with me. After that first year, he was fine and enjoyed being with the older boys. They always seemed to have a great time. Sue would come on Thursday, and the parents would come up on Friday night for the weekend. They would take the boys home and leave the girls for their week with Grandpa and sometimes Grandma.

Our five granddaughters were all born within three years of one another. The routine was pretty much the same for the girls as it was for the boys. They would play all kinds of games, like hide and go seek, play in the lake, go swimming and fishing, sit around the campfire and talk about girl things. There was a merry-go-round just across from the trailer that they loved to play on. Occasionally we would go into town for something, and I would take them to the Dairy Queen. It was a wonderful time.

As the grandchildren grew older, it became harder and harder for all of them to get together at the same time. One would work, another one would have to babysit, and a couple of them were in dance line at school. Their time was pretty well spoken for. Those great times became a memory and something to long for. It gradually became harder for me to take the pontoon out by myself to go fishing, and we decided to sell the trailer. It had been great fun while we had it, and everyone enjoyed it, but everything has a season. We put a FOR SALE sign in the window on a Saturday, and someone came along on Sunday and bought it. We were all very happy and had four years of enjoyment and many lasting memories.

Now all of the grandchildren are adults. At Christmas 2006, we overheard them reminiscing about the good times they shared on their annual week at the lake with Grandpa and the good meals he would make for them.

I continued to have problems with my leg, and I decided to see my orthopedic surgeon who referred me to Rochester for another total hip replacement. In the spring of 1996, I was told that the surgery would probably be the last one I would be able to have due to the condition of the bone structure in my leg. They took out everything that had been in place and totally reconstructed the hip with a new prosthesis. I was at home in bed within five days after my surgery. I had home care and physical therapy for about a month before I could function without any further assistance.

Since I had sold the trailer, I needed to find something to occupy my time and get me out of the house. Willard had a relative that had a used car lot in St. Cloud. I would go over and help him and just hang out. We would go to car auctions together, and he taught me the used-car business. I would buy a car here and there and then sell it and make a few dollars.

THIRTY

Counselor Employment

In 1998 I got a call from the director of Recovery Plus at St. Cloud Hospital. He needed a temporary van driver to help transport adolescents back and forth to treatment. I agreed to help him, and it was about three months before they were able to hire a permanent van driver. I knew that due to my physical disabilities, I would not be able to drive a truck again. Because I had previous chemical dependency counselor training and experience, I asked the clinical supervisor if he would keep me in mind if a counselor position opened up.

A short time later, a position opened for a part-time counselor for Recovery Plus Unit, and I was hired. I was thrilled at the opportunity and believed, if I could get my foot in the door, I could possibly handle a full-time job later on, even though I had physical limitations. I was given whatever time I needed to familiarize myself with the changes that had taken place in the field and to brush up on the latest rules, laws, documentation, treatment, and policies of the unit. It was about a week before I started helping out in the seniors program and other out-patient programs. I was part time for about a month, and I found I was working forty hours or more every week and was put on full-time status, making me eligible for hospital benefits.

When I returned to work at Recovery Plus, counselors were not required to be licensed because Recovery Plus was a teaching facility and hospital based. Therefore, the hospital employees were exempt from chemical dependency licensure. I knew that, eventually, all counselors in the field would need to be licensed, and since I had the required hours, training, and experience, I applied to be grandfathered in as a Licensed Alcohol and Drug Counselor (LADC). I was granted this license by the Department of Health of the State of Minnesota. I became an active member in the Minnesota Association of Resources for Recovery and Chemical Health (MARRCH). I served on the MARRCH board as a representative from our district in 1998 and served as a member of the Public Policy Committee from 1999 until 2007.

The latter part of 2001, I became aware of the availability of funds to help train professional counselors for licensure as gambling addiction counselors. I approached the program director of Recovery Plus and asked if he would be interested in starting a gambling addiction program. I knew there certainly was a need for it, and I also knew I would be able to obtain the funds to train the staff, enabling them to become licensed to treat people for gambling addiction.

He agreed and gave me permission to go ahead and put a program together. I was to select the staff for training and schedule the training. I interviewed staff that I thought might be interested, and most of them agreed to undergo sixty hours of classroom training required for licensure. After approximately two months, I had the team formed and trained. We began to market a gambling addiction program and notified staff throughout the hospital that Recovery Plus Gambling Addiction Program would be able to accommodate referrals for the patients. Within six months of operation we had twelve people in the program.

The annual MARRCH Conference is held in October at the Riverside Center in St. Paul, Minnesota. It is a three and a half day statewide conference with nationally known speakers in the field of addiction. The conference usually draws between 1,200 and 1,400 people. About ten consecutive workshops are held for the professionals to obtain Continuing Education Credits (CEU's) required for continued licensure in the State of Minnesota.

Each year someone is chosen from nominations submitted from agencies throughout the state to be counselor of the year. This person is selected by a nominating committee formed by the MARRCH Board. Much to my surprise, in 2003 my name was submitted for this award by a dear friend from Recovery Plus. I was chosen by the committee to receive the certificate of honor by being selected as "Counselor of the Year, 2003."

Sue and our daughters had been notified and planned to attend the ceremony to surprise me. During the night, Sue became ill and was taken to the hospital. Karen stayed in St. Cloud with Sue, but, to my surprise, Cindy and Sharon attended the event. It was a great honor for me; one I'll never forget. The only thing missing was that Sue couldn't be there to share it with me. I was anxious and concerned until I could get back to St. Cloud to make sure Sue was all right. She came home the following day, and we celebrated my award.

In 2003, I was selected by the Department of Health for the State of Minnesota to administer the oral portion of the exam for LADC licensure.

In the fall of 2004, my leg started to deteriorate again, and my breathing was becoming more of a problem. I knew it was time to turn the gambling addiction program over to a co-worker of mine whom I highly respected. I approached the program director and let him know what I had in mind, and he agreed that it was time to let someone take over the reins. I continued to do some promotional work for the gambling program throughout the community.

I also continued to help administer the LADC exams for the state until Minnesota handed over that responsibility to the governor's office in 2005, and a new Board of Behavioral Health and Therapy (BBHT) was created. I applied for and was appointed to the BBHT by the governor of the State of Minnesota in the latter part of 2005. I took my seat on the board in January of 2006 and was assigned to the Conflict Resolution Committee. This committee works to expedite and resolve complaints against counselors and facilities that had allegedly broken the rules of professional conduct.

I often sat in awe and wonder, when I thought about the appointment to a board such as BBHT. As I looked around the table I saw people with no less than a master's degree, with doctorates, psychologists, and here I sat at the same table with two and a half years of formal education chemical dependency counselor training and continuing education workshops. I sometimes asked myself, "What are you doing here?" Then I had to remind myself, if I wasn't qualified, I wouldn't be there.

Fifth Generation, 2006
Left to right, seated: Erica, Millie holding Jakob; standing: Cindy, Sue, and John.

THIRTY-ONE

Glorious Golden Wedding Anniversary

In the summer of 2006, we began talking to Sue's extended family in Richmond, Virginia, about our fiftieth wedding anniversary, which we would be celebrating in 2007. We began planning a celebration to take place during the summer (Virginians don't like the cold weather) and began getting commitments from relatives to come for the anniversary gathering. There were thirteen relatives who made reservations for the week, as well as our children and their spouses. The grandchildren and their significant others would come as they could. We rented two places on Breezy Point near Brainerd, Minnesota, and took a year to plan for this week of celebration. We were expecting to have a great time.

Our actual anniversary was March 8, 2007, when we celebrated fifty years of marriage. We had so many wonderful friends who played an important part in our lives that we wanted them to celebrate with us. We decided to have a fiftieth wedding anniversary celebration on March 11th for our friends in Minnesota who weren't afraid of the cold weather. Since we were planning to have our Virginia family here during the summer, we did not plan for them to come in March.

Fiftieth Wedding Anniversary, March 8, 2007.

Two weeks before our celebration, I was continuing to have more problems breathing and was told by my pulmonary physician that I would need to be on oxygen around-the-clock. This was quite a shock to Sue and me, and we were both down-hearted. We called Sue's sister, Gail, to share the news. During our conversation she could pick up on our depression. She hung

Our fiftieth anniversary in the Virginia newspaper. Left to right, seated: Sue and John; standing: Don and Gail Bruch, Bill and Carol Antone, Ann and Fred Antone, Sue's siblings.

up the phone and got the family together for the greatest surprise of our lives.

The day before the anniversary celebration on March 11, Karen called to say she was having a surprise gathering for our granddaughter and would we come. Once we arrived, we were surprised that we were the only people there. We asked where everyone was. Karen said that John's parents were running a bit late and told us that Sue's family from Virginia sent a greeting she wanted to play for us before the surprise party began. A CD began to play (or so we thought) with beautiful singing, and it was definitely Sue's family singing. As we turned our heads, up the stairs came Sue's sister and her husband, Don, her brother Fred and his wife, Ann, and her brother, Bill, and his wife, Carol. They were singing their greeting in person. Tears of surprise and joy were shed by all. When Sue's siblings found out that I had gotten the news about having to be on oxygen twenty-four-seven, they knew they needed to be here to cheer us up.

It was the most wonderful surprise. We cried, laughed, told stories and had the greatest time that day. Our kids and Sue's siblings and spouses had partied in Prior Lake when they arrived on Friday before coming to St. Cloud to party with us on Saturday. Sunday, March 11, was the big day with the rest of our friends. Karen and her husband, John, put together a slide show that would play all afternoon. There were about 150 guests to celebrate with us.

Sue's sister and brother-in-law stayed for an extra week, and her brothers and their spouses flew back home on Monday. Then all of them came back in three months for the big family celebration that had been planned for a year. Talk about dedication and love.

By mid November 2007, it had become increasingly more difficult to continue working, even a few hours at a time. I was using oxygen around the clock, and I also needed my motorized scooter at work to preserve my leg. The doctors said that my chance of surviving another surgery would only be about ten percent due to lung deterioration and the chance of infection. I had to ask myself the question, "Why am I working? Am I hanging on? If I am, why?" I really didn't have an answer.

I had also seen my physician at the VA Hospital who said that I was like a cat with nine lives and had out-lived eight and a half of them. He informed me that I was in the end stages of emphysema. He also told me if there was any way possible for me to get away from Minnesota, into a warmer climate for the winter months, I should do so because the cold weather would be very hard on me. After hearing that, I made the decision to retire completely. Sue was relieved as she had been trying to get me to retire for some time. I called the clinical supervisor and told her of my plan and sent in my resignation.

In 2007, I had been reappointed to BBHT and the Conflict Resolution Committee. I also sent an e-mail to the Board of

John and Sue at John's retirement party, July 2007.

Behavioral Health and Therapy, informing them that due to my medical condition I would sadly have to resign from the board effective November 15, 2007, which was the final board meeting of the year.

THIRTY-TWO

With Grateful Hearts

As I look at my life and ponder my existence on this earth, I ask God, "Are you finished with me yet?" God has been good. He has watched over us, has guided my life even when I was far away from him. I understand that he has always been there and that it is me who has been moving away. He has blessed Sue and me with three wonderful children, eight beautiful grandchildren, and so far, one beautiful great-grandson. We are proud of them all. Our grandchildren are beginning to get married and starting a whole new generation. We have been blessed with Sue's extended family and with my step-family and many wonderful friends throughout the years.

I thank God for helping Sue and me believe in each other. God has given us the grace to honor our marriage vows. I love Sue with all my heart, and when I look back on our life together, I realize there have been many times when we have faltered and hurt one another and had to ask for forgiveness and have had to forgive. Even now, I am tempted to ask for Sue's forgiveness. Yet when I reflect on that, I say to myself, "If it were not for all those times when the hours seemed to be the darkest and we had little hope that our marriage would survive, we maybe wouldn't have continued to work on it and put our trust in God. We took one day at a time, put one foot in front of the other, and, gradually over the years, we learned to love one another deeply. Because it was hard and there were many painful times in some periods of our life, that is what brought us to the true meaning of love. Then, it is with gratitude and thanks that I say to the God of my understanding, "Thank You," for having brought Sue into my life and having taught us the meaning of true love.

Epilogue

John died before his book could be published after living with one lung and struggling with emphysema for fourteen years. He had completed the story that was originally to be an account of his life for his children and grandchildren. As he shared his story with other people, they encouraged him to write a book. In the end, his choice was to do just that. The book went to the publisher about a week before he entered the hospital for the last time on August 15, 2008.

While in the hospital John began to talk about the process of dying. He spoke as if he were directing a play. As different caregivers would enter his room, he would share with us who the players were. The first player was the physician who with great compassion and honesty shared with us that John's condition was terminal, and he would have but a few months, possibly weeks, to live. The next player was his night nurse whom he called his "angel" as she treated him with empathy and love. Another player was the chaplain who anointed him late in the evening. The following day, we had requested a meeting with the hospice team, which consisted of a different chaplain, the physician, a social worker, and the hospice nurse. As John shared parts of his story with them, you could see tears in some of their eyes. After consultation with the hospice team and the decision was made to return home with hospice, the team left. John asked us to come closer as he turned his hands upward and said: "God if it be your will and you are finished with me, than I am ready."

We took John home on Tuesday, August 19th around 5:00 p.m. On Wednesday, the hospice nurse came and spent an hour or so with him and told him she would be back on Friday. She too was one of the players. Earlier in the day he had asked for his granddaughter, Diane, who came with her fiancé, Josh, that evening. He signed the draft copy of his book for her as a wedding gift and, after she and Josh left, he called a family meeting. Sharon, Karen, Cindy, and I were present. He told us how important his family had always been and how much he loved us. On Thursday August 21st the hospice certified nurse assistant came to help with John. She was very kind and gentle with him, before she left, he told her she was another one of the players and that there was one player left. On Friday, August 22, 2008, he died peacefully with us at his side. We do not know who the final player was, perhaps it was God.

John's Family, "The loves of his life."

ACKNOWLEDGEMENTS

For many years, friends and acquaintances have been urging me to document my experiences. I had resisted their efforts because I had almost destroyed my life and the lives of my family fighting the many memories and experiences of my child hood and a good part of my adult life. My wife, Sue, and children, Sharon, Karen, and Cindy asked me questions about my history and stories about when I was a child. For the most part, I avoided going into detail, not wanting to relive those early years. As the children grew up and started raising families of their own and their children started asking questions, I had to decide if I was willing to give them a missing piece of their history. By that time I had been on a path of recovery from my own addiction for thirty-five years and had made sufficient progress in my recovery so as not focus on my past, rather share my past as an act of love to my family.

As the grandchildren progressed into the teen years, I was asked to give a few presentations to their classes in school. I was asked to talk about my childhood and some of my experiences growing up as an orphan in a war-torn country and my eventual journey to the United States as a stowaway on an American ship. To this day, I consider it a privilege and honor that the grandchildren thought my story worthy to share with their classmates.

I apologize in advance to anyone who gave me encouragement along the way and whose name has been omitted. The memory is no longer as sharp as it once was.

First, I want to thank the Willard Van Vickle family, for this book would not have been published had Willard and Millie, Robert and Sylvia (mother and father of Willard) not tried every avenue open to them including writing a letter to then President Harry Truman to gain my release from Ellis Island to their care. The acceptance into their family system and the acceptance by the extended family taught me what love without reservation is all about. To this day, I consider Willard and Millie's two children, Rocky and Randy, my brothers.

To my wife, Sue, and our daughters Sharon, Karen, and Cindy for not giving up on me and continually urging me to get the story written. Thank you for helping to open my eyes and my heart. Initially, the importance of having that piece of history documented for our children just didn't sink in.

To our grandchildren: Michael, Joshua, Katie, Maranda, Diane, Jackie, Erica, and Nathan. Thank you for all the joy you have brought to my life and the good times we have shared throughout the years. Above all, the joy we experienced on our annual week-long camping trips. As adults you have continued to encourage me to get my history written, and here it is.

To my sons-in-law, Steve, Jake, and Martin. Thank you, for being there for our support and the support of our daughters. You have loved us with our flaws and accepted us as your family. We appreciate the time spent with us and making yourselves available when needed.

To our extended family—Don and Gail Bruch, Fred and Ann Antone and Bill and Carol Antone and their families in Richmond, Virginia—for all of the prayers and support as well as their friendship over the years. We have had many fun times and laughs. Thank you and know you are loved and close to our hearts.

To Peter T. Honer, my friend who helped me through treatment as my counselor and years later as a co-worker. He has been there over the years to give our family direction when we had difficulty staying on course. Just knowing you are there is a comfort to everyone in the family. Having you as our friend is a Blessing.

To Doug Greenlee, a colleague and dear friend, who kept after me to make a record of my life. His persistence, encouragement and enthusiasm kept me focused and moving forward when exposing painful areas of my life.

Dee Dee Bruyere, a colleague, friend, and mentor. Dee Dee and I spent many hours discussing and solving the world's problems. I don't understand why nothing has changed. We shared the good times as well as the difficult times in our lives and trusted each others opinions. Thanks for being my friend.

Claire Bauer, a long-standing friend who was the first person to interview me on video tape in an attempt to get my story recorded as a historical record for our children and grandchildren. Thank you. Words alone are not enough.

Thanks Emily Stessman for all your hard work transcribing the tapes into a rough draft of this book. I know at times, due to my breathing, it was hard to make out what I was saying on the tape. Your dedication to this project and time spent on this book was invaluable. It was such a privilege meeting you and sharing a meal.

To Dave De Mars, thanks for helping us get started and making the initial contact with us to the publisher. You helped us in understanding the publishing process and becoming comfortable in what we were undertaking. You and Linda hold special places in our hearts.

To Sr. Janice Wedl, OSB, who courageously agreed to undertake the job of editing this book. In spite of having to endure an unexpected illness and hospitalization with a long period of recovery, she refused to give up and insisted on finishing the book. She took my writings, reading and re-reading them and put them in an order that made sense, not once becoming upset with the quality of my work. Sr. Janice encouraged me to continue when I felt like giving up and assured me the book was worth completing.

Sr. Linda Kulzer, OSB, Sue's friend, who agreed to help us get the story dictated and made ready for the editor. Thank you, Linda, for meeting with us weekly, giving direction for content and providing guidance for the coming week's dictation. Without her nudge, it would have taken us an additional six to twelve months trying to get the book on tape and transcribed. Many thanks for your encouragement and friendship. We have been blessed having you become a part of our story and forevermore consider you are a part of this book and our family.

To Jim Forsting, my boss! I am proud to call him my friend who truly cares and takes an interest in the lives of the people he works with and allows them to achieve their full potential. Thank you, Jim, for caring; it shows in everything you do.

To my wife, Sue, a special thank you for helping with the preparation of this book. With gratitude and love for matching me stride for stride in the life we lived with its ups and downs, bringing us to this point in our lives where the words Thank you and I love you just are not enough. Forever Yours, John.

A special Thank You to the staff of Centra Care Health Systems, Recovery Plus, past and present. First for accepting me for treatment and later encouraging me to apply for training as a Alcohol and Drug Counselor. The staff over the years have become an extended family and played a big part in helping me grow personally and professionally until my retirement in 2007. You all deserve a huge THANK YOU for the work you do, the lives you help save and the family systems you help teach to cope and heal.